A BEGINNER'S
Guide

TO THE ESSENTIALS

of

INVESTING

Learn the basics of investing, avoid costly retirement mistakes, and improve upon your current investments.

A BEGINNER'S

Guide

TO THE ESSENTIALS

of

INVESTING

Matthew Scott Freye

Barbara!
Happy Investing
&
Happy Reading!

Published by Matthew Freye. Illustrations by Josey Malayil. Editing by Gillian Autton and Angela Bates. Cover work by Faith Luke.

Book layout, cover art and design created and copyrighted © 2017 by Matthew Freye.

Contact: info@ifreye.com
www.ifreye.com

ISBN-13: 978-1-5219-3853-9

Printed in the United States of America.

"An investment in knowledge
pays the best interest."

Benjamin Franklin

Table of Contents

Preface

Of the numerous groups of investors from all walks of life and socioeconomic backgrounds that I have worked with, one common theme I've noticed is an overall lack of knowledge regarding the fundamentals of investing. People generally just don't understand it. The world of finance and investing often conjures up notions of wonderment. A world of intrigue and complexities, where the elites gather – not the common folk. I get it. I was once there, too!

Investing affects all of us to some extent, whether in the form of a 401(k) for our retirement savings or a college savings account for our children. While you can get away with not understanding the fundamentals of investing, you're better off knowing where you're putting your money and what it's doing there.

What are these accounts? How do they work? What are the basics of investing? The answers to these questions are really not difficult to find, but oftentimes the information is presented to us in a way that turns us off – statistics coupled with complex stock charts and interest rate discussions, presented in a formal, collegiate way. That's not very fun for most people. But it doesn't have to be that way.

In my junior year of college, the world of finance intrigued me so much that I made the decision to switch my major from Architecture to Finance. As I finished my degree, I worked two jobs – one was with a leading brokerage firm and the other was with a leading bank. Soon after graduating college with a Bachelor's of Science in Finance, I started working full-time in brokerage houses and have now been in this industry for almost twenty years. During my career, I have worked for quite a few of our nation's largest and most well-known brokerage firms in various capacities – an invaluable experience. I have been exposed to how different firms operate and approach investing, and I have witnessed first-hand the inner workings of the brokerage industry.

When I first started working with clients, I was fresh out of college, and the theories and formulas I had spent years studying were still fresh in my mind. I would often interject the theories I mastered in college while discussing personal finances with clients. I would explain complex formulas as to how we arrived at the figures we did and go into great detail about concepts that went way over their heads. Sure, I probably sounded intelligent and they were impressed, but did they truly understand their own investments? Heck, did they even understand what I was saying?

On this note, I remember working with many wives who, when the topic of finances came up, would immediately direct me to their husbands as if they were the financial bearers of the household. I get it, these are the traditional roles society has put us in. The thing is, when I spoke with their husbands, the husbands didn't even know the basics. Sure, they acted as if they did, but as I probed further, neither one of the couple really understood their personal finances. It was not enough that my clients agreed with what I said. Of more importance to me was that my clients actually became educated and understood what I was recommending to them and why.

In order to determine whether or not they were actually learning from our meetings, I would pose questions to them based on our conversations. Essentially, the spotlight was now on them to explain to me what I had just discussed with them. That's when the nodding of the heads stopped and the fidgeting and the "umms" started flowing like water.

Clients would often feel comfortable just knowing that someone like me was "watching over" their investments. That was not good enough for me though. I wanted more for, and expected more from, my clients; and I want and expect the same from you! It was my goal that they become active participants in their own financial lives if even just by understanding the basics of investing. I soon learned one of the best ways to achieve this goal was for me to explain investing concepts in simpler terms. Not to insult my clients, but to present the material in such a way that they would actually understand and retain the information. Time after time, my approach received rave reviews, and I was frequently told that I should write a book to reach many more people. Well, that is exactly what I have done.

The concepts I will present to you in this book may be complex and can seem quite daunting. However, understanding the basics, which is a first step, doesn't have to be so challenging. I will attempt to keep things simple by starting off with very basic discussions surrounding investments, and then as we progress through the chapters, we will introduce more complex ideas. I will also highlight important terms that will broaden your financial literacy. Worry not, my goal is to hold your hand through this process and gently guide you on through to more complex investing ideas. On this note, I would suggest that you read this book in the order presented. You may have an interest in learning the basics of 401(k)s and decide to jump to Chapter 11, and that is great, but to truly benefit from this book, start with Chapter 1 and advance in order.

Introduction

Whether knocking on the doors of my neighbors offering to do their yard work for a few dollars or peddling my bike through the rain on my first paper route, I have held a job since about age nine. The money I earned was deposited into a savings account that my parents had opened up for me at an early age. By the time I was eighteen I had managed to put a few thousand dollars into that savings account. The thing is, each month, I realized, the account only provided me pennies in interest. It was extremely disheartening to see my hard-earned dollars earn next to nothing. I had to believe, or at least hope, there was a better way to invest my savings so that they could grow more substantially.

I looked up various financial advisors and investment brokers listed in the phone book and decided to call a few of them. After all, these types of professionals could at least guide me on the right path to learning about investing, right? I mean, they could at least spend a few moments with me on the phone or recommend a book for me to read, right? No. Professionals they were not.

Once they found out my age and the fact that I didn't have a lot of money (although a few thousand dollars was, and still is, a lot of money to me), I was essentially laughed at and mocked. Often, they would simply hang up on me. Any ego I might have had was quickly squashed. Undeterred, I took matters into my own hands and ventured down to the local library (this was prior to the internet) and checked out books related to investing, in particular beginning investing.

The thing is, the books about investing – even the so-called beginner books – were way over my head. They would either jump straight into explaining how to trade stocks or they would present complex investing principals and theories. I learned very little, if anything at all, and once again, humility and reality set in that this investing thing may not be for me. But I was determined to learn more and continued on with my research.

I went so far as to buy finance newspapers in hopes of garnering some type of investment knowledge. These would often devote pages and pages to explaining what, at the time for me, were complex ideas about the economy, interest rates, drug companies, tech companies, and even international financial news. There would even be dozens of pages with nothing more than hundreds if not thousands of stock ticker listings.

Day after day, many of the same stock tickers would be shown with arrows indicating an increase or decrease in price from the prior day coupled with point or percentage indicators. I even recognized a few of the stock tickers as representing well-known companies like T for AT&T® and IBM for, well, IBM®.

As I sat there holding the money and investing sections open, perusing through the hundreds of stock tickers, I felt as though people looking at me must think I was a sophisticated guy, and I may have even gotten a little ego boost from this. Trust me when I tell you that I had no idea what I was looking at, and I certainly did not have any money invested in these stocks.

Combine this confusing listing of stocks and the so-called "beginner" books on investing with the fact that I was laughed at by real-world investment professionals, and you can imagine that I was at a loss. I had no idea what to do. I felt intimated and, frankly, I started to think this investing thing is for those with money and Ivy League degrees.

So, why do I share all of this with you? After all, I'm supposed to be building some authority that I know what I am talking about. Well, I want you to know that I was in the same boat as I imagine many of you are sitting in right now. I thought this investing thing was just not for me.

A few years into my collegiate studies, I decided to switch majors from architecture to business with a specialty in finance. Not only did I earn a Bachelor's of Science in Finance, but during college I worked at one of the largest national banks in the U.S. and held a second job with one of our nation's largest brokerage firms. By this time I was learning about investing and gaining real-world experience working with some of our nation's largest and oldest investment firms.

Pretty soon, I was working in the same field as those gentleman who, only a few years earlier, had mocked me. And I wanted to make damn sure that I never treated anyone the way I was treated.

Chapter 1

The Buckets

Let's start off our discussion with what I hope you will find to be an entertaining case in point. I want you to imagine that you have just won $10 million playing the local Powerball lottery. Not only that, but you have no debt and no financial obligations and can do whatever you want with these new winnings. Perhaps you decide to splurge a bit of the winnings on a new car or expensive watch or whatever it is that you fancy. With the remaining amount, however, you decide to invest your winnings. But what types of investments are out there?

Please take a moment to contemplate the types of investments you think you would be able to place your winnings into.

From my professional experience working with clients and in my own personal experience, I imagine your list would include some or all of the following:

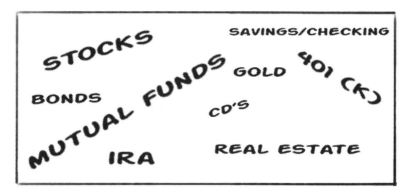

Does your list include any of the above items? Don't worry if it doesn't, these are just the items I have commonly heard listed as investments.

RISK: UNCERTAINTY OF A RETURN AND THE POTENTIAL FOR FINANCIAL LOSS.

In reality, you will have numerous investments to choose from, each with their own distinct risk levels, costs, tax consequences, return probabilities, and so forth. The list is by no means exhaustive. In fact, some of the items listed are not even investments in and of themselves; they are simply accounts that, without investments inside them, will do nothing for you investment-wise.

Some of the items listed that *are* investments may present extreme amounts of risk, while others not so much. Some of the investments may require thousands of dollars to initially invest in, while others may require just a minimal investment amount. No wonder the world of investing seems so perplexing. Let's start to clear things up together.

I am going to ask that for now you forget all of your preconceived notions regarding the types of investments that are available to you. Instead, I am going to ask that you imagine three buckets, each with their respective label of *Cash*, *Bonds*, and *Stocks*:

Yup, it's that simple! There may be certain types of investments that many of us have heard of through radio programming and television commercials, such as real estate and gold, but from my experience, these are usually outlier-type investments; I am going to ask that you not concern yourself with them for the time being. For now, keep it as simple as I have laid out for you in the above illustration.

The next few chapters are devoted to examining each of the buckets. By the end of each chapter, you'll know which types of investments are in each bucket and their corresponding risks and rewards. We will start off with basic discussions and, as our journey progresses, we will gradually introduce more complex investing concepts and discuss how the buckets are interwoven in other areas of investing – such as 401(k)s. This approach provides the most educational experience.

Chapter 2

The Cash Bucket

Let us begin our discussion of the *cash bucket* with a high-level overview of what may seem like a very elementary example – checking accounts.

Checking Accounts

Most of us, at one point in our lives, have held a job that provided a paycheck. You probably used this paycheck to pay bills, buy groceries, and perhaps spend a bit on luxury items (e.g., TVs, iPads, and the like). You probably don't simply cash your paychecks and hoard the cash, stashing it in a safe or burying it in secret spots throughout your property. I imagine at some point in time, you've had a checking account where you deposited those paychecks.

You usually have access to the funds in a number of ways, including a checkbook, debit card, and online payment features. But, why would we use a checking account as opposed to hoarding our cash at home or burying it in secret spots? The answer may seem obvious, but let's briefly discuss the potential reasons.

RETURN: THE BENEFIT TO AN INVESTOR RESULTING FROM AN INVESTMENT OF SOME RESOURCE.

It is probably evident to a good majority of us that hoarding money in our homes or burying it throughout our property carries with it tremendous risk. Perhaps there is a fire, theft, or maybe we even forget where we hid the money. When bills come due (e.g., power, mortgage, rent), you're usually unable to pay those bills with physical cash. When is the last time you can think of a mortgage company accepting a cash payment?

But perhaps more importantly is that by hoarding your money or burying it throughout your property, assuming no nefarious activities occur, your money will not grow in size over time. It will not earn a return.

Practical experience suggests that opening a checking account is a rather straightforward and easy process. Large national banks and even small local banks usually have very little, if any, minimum balance requirements for opening a checking account, which means most people can open one, whether we have a few hundred dollars (or less) or we have millions of dollars. Not only are checking accounts accessible, but once opened and funded, checking accounts provide us *liquidity*.

Liquidity is an important financial term and essentially describes how easy it is to convert assets into cash. That is to say, that with a checking account, you are usually provided debit cards, checkbooks, and online payment options, sometimes at no cost. All of these are features that allow you immediate access to your money.

LIQUIDITY: HOW EASY IT IS TO CONVERT ASSETS INTO CASH.

Additionally, although this can change, there is usually little to no fee for having a checking account open. Sure, there may be fees for ordering additional checkbooks or duplicate tax documents, but by in large there are no fees for simply having a checking account opened and funded. In essence, a checking account is an affordable and very *liquid* account to deposit money into.

Liquidity

One very important aspect of cash investments is the idea of liquidity. Liquidity entails having access to your money rather quickly. For example, with a debit card tied to a checking account, you have the ability to withdraw cash from ATMs. If you needed cash for an item you saw at a garage sale, you could go to an ATM and withdraw cash immediately. That same debit card can also be used directly at point-of-sale, such as swiping the card at the grocery store checkout lane. Additionally, you can usually plug your card number into an online shopping cart, such as Amazon, and purchase goods and services immediately.

Compare this sort of liquidity to that of selling a home. If you need the cash you've invested into your home (excluding anything like home equity lines of credit), it could potentially take months or years before you get your hands on the cash because you have to first put the house up for sale, then wait for a buyer, sign contracts, wait for the money to be wired, etc. This would generally be considered *illiquid*.

FDIC Insurance

I mentioned earlier that hoarding cash at home or burying it may pose a great amount of risk (e.g., forget where you buried it or a fire consumes it) and that checking accounts may be a better alternative. However, are there risks with having your money in a checking account? Sure. One risk would be that the bank you opened your account with goes out of business for any number of reasons. So what happens to your money then?

Another feature of checking accounts held at U.S. banking institutions is the Federal Deposit Insurance Corporation (or FDIC) insurance. FDIC deposit insurance enables consumers to confidently place their money at thousands of FDIC-insured banks across the country, and is backed by the full faith and credit of the United States government. The standard insurance amount is $250,000 per depositor, per insured bank, for each account ownership category.[1] Meaning that any amount of money you deposit into one category of checking accounts at each bank, up to $250,000, is insured by the FDIC and that if something were to happen at your bank (they went out of business, say), you would be guaranteed to recover that amount.

So, checking accounts often times have low to no balance requirements, low to non-existent fees, the ability to access your money on demand (i.e., *liquidity*), and can be covered by FDIC insurance. As such, by depositing money into a checking account, you are not taking on a lot of risk when compared to other investments that we will cover in later chapters. So, would you expect to receive a lot of interest on your checking account deposits? Hopefully not, and in reality, checking accounts usually pay minimal interest. After all, a checking account is simply a place for you to "park" or house your money for the time being.

Let's look at some other investments that may earn us more return.

Savings Accounts

Another common bank product I imagine most people are familiar with is a savings account, which is often times opened at the same bank you open your checking account with. Although at first glance, checking and savings accounts may seem similar, there are some distinct differences. First of all, unlike a good portion of checking accounts, savings accounts will usually have higher initial, and perhaps ongoing, balance requirements. Whereas with a checking account you may be able to deposit just a few dollars at account opening, savings accounts may require a few hundred or even a few thousand dollars to open and may also require that you maintain a minimum balance. This particular feature might make it a bit harder to invest in.

The liquidity of savings accounts when compared to other, more risky investments, which will be covered in later chapters, is decent. However, when compared to checking accounts, there is a noticeable lack of liquidity. For example, savings accounts generally do not offer

---

1   Source: www.fdic.gov

a debit card feature. This means you will not usually be able to use the money in your savings account for online purchases or at points-of-sale such as at the grocery store checkout line, nor through ATM withdrawals. However, savings accounts may offer check capabilities (i.e., a checkbook), but usually checks written off of a savings account must be written for at least a minimum amount (e.g., $250). Granted, the check writing feature of a savings account does provide liquidity, but not as much liquidity as with a checking account.

One potential benefit of a savings account is that it will fall under the same insurance as that of a checking account. That is, savings accounts will be covered by FDIC insurance. So, even though your liquidity has decreased when compared to a checking account, you still have some assurance that the money in your savings account will still be there in the event of a bank failure (subjected to FDIC limits). However, because you have taken on additional *risk* (i.e., less liquidity) as well as having to adhere to more stringent requirements (e.g., minimum balances) you can expect to earn more interest on the money in a savings account when compared to checking accounts. Albeit, the rates on both checking and savings accounts are usually rather low, and some would even say preposterously low. Nonetheless, we are earning something on our money when compared to the alternatives – burying our cash or hoarding onto it.

At this point, some of you may regret purchasing this book because these examples seem so elementary. "I already know this!" you might exclaim. Bear with me because there is a method to this madness. With that said, let's discuss another cash investment that is a step-up in risk when compared to checking and savings accounts.

Certificates of Deposit (CDs)

I imagine a majority of you have heard about and perhaps even have experience with CDs. CD stands for *Certificate of Deposit* and is also commonly purchased at your local banking institution. One main difference when investing in a CD is that there are required initial investment amounts and they can vary greatly ranging anywhere from $1,000 to hundreds of thousands of dollars. Whereas checking and savings accounts may have little to no minimum balance requirements, CDs usually have these much higher investment amounts and that may mean some of us will not be able to participate in them. Additionally, CDs are issued with *maturities,* and these maturity periods can vary greatly ranging anywhere from less than one year to upwards of multiple years (e.g., three months, one year, five year, etc.).

Essentially, the way a CD works is you choose the amount you want to invest (based on the minimum requirements set forth by the CD) and a maturity period. Then, your money is "locked-up" for that period. Once the maturity period is reached, you should expect to receive your initial investment back, along with any stated interest. With this in mind, let's imagine that you have invested in a six-month CD and in month three you need to access those funds – could you? After all, we just learned that your money is "locked-up" for the maturity period.

Often, there are caveats that allow you to access your money before the set maturity period, but usually in these instances you will be expected to pay a fee and you may be assessed

MATURITY: THE DATE ON WHICH THE PRINCIPAL IS RETURNED TO AN INVESTOR.

a penalty on top of that fee.[2] For example, let's assume you invested $1,000 in the six-month CD and in month three you withdraw your funds. Perhaps your bank will charge you a $100 early termination fee. As a result, you would only receive $900 back. In this instance, you have actually lost money. This potential to lose money in a CD presents us with much more risk when compared to checking or savings accounts, and as a result, you should expect (no, you should demand) to receive a higher interest rate. After all, you are taking on more risk, and when we take on more risk, we should expect more return. It is worth noting, that CDs purchased at a U.S. banking institution will generally also be covered by the same FDIC insurance that covers checking and savings accounts.[3]

---

2   The fees and/or penalties charged on early withdrawals may vary greatly depending on the financial institution. Please check with your financial institution prior to making any investment decisions.

3   FDIC insurance may not apply to brokered CDs, which are purchased through a brokerage account.

I realize it may seem that I am presenting only the bad when it comes to investments, especially CDs. My intention is to present you both the potential risks and the rewards, so that you know what you are getting into. I can recall numerous instances when clients would invest in a CD and need to withdraw the money early. Their bank would charge an early withdrawal fee or "penalty." I have seen this play out time and again with clients. They simply did not know what they were getting into (the basics) and felt it was unfair to be charged the early withdrawal fee. I get it, I really do. It does not necessarily sound fair, but that's how this particular investment vehicle works.

On a more positive note, CDs can play an important role in an investment portfolio. For example, let's assume that you have $5,000 that you are looking to invest and you are relatively certain you will not need to use that money for eight months. You could simply leave the money in a checking or savings account, but an eight-month CD might also be an option that pays a substantially higher rate of return (i.e., interest)—more "bang for your buck." Hopefully, you are starting to see that you need to weigh the risks and rewards of these investment vehicles and determine what suits you the best. Sure, a checking account is an option and you will have access to the money whenever you need it, but by taking on a bit more risk in a CD (e.g., money being locked up for the maturity period) you could potentially earn a higher interest rate.

Ultimately, what I hope you are beginning to see is that to make more return on your money (in this instance, interest), you will need to be willing to take on more risk. This is a fundamental concept when it comes to investing.

On this note, the below chart depicts the various cash investments we have discussed thus far, along with their average interest rates, and should solidify this basic concept of investing.

Table 1.1 - Interest Rates for the Years 2000, 2006 and 2016.

Investment	January 5, 2000 (%)	January 4, 2006 (%)	January 6, 2016 (%)
Checking Account	1.75	1.11	0.01
Savings Account	2.01	1.91	0.09
Six-month CD	4.63	2.84	0.16

Source: Bankrate.com

In 2000 and 2006, investments in a six-month CD would have earned you almost three times as much interest as a checking account. But remember, with the six-month CD you are taking on additional risk and this is why you would expect to earn more interest. After all, with the CD you are *locking up* your money for a set maturity period, unlike checking or savings accounts, which have no maturity period.

We started our discussion by introducing the topic of checking accounts and then gradually introduced riskier investments (e.g., savings accounts and CDs). We will now introduce another cash investment that may present more risks, but also potentially more return.

Money Market Mutual Fund

Unlike checking accounts, savings accounts, and CDs, Money Market Mutual Funds (MMMF)[4] are usually only offered through a brokerage account, which is different from a bank account (more on this in Chapter 12). However, if your local bank offers brokerage services (and many do), then you may be able to access a Money Market Mutual Fund through that brokerage account. Unlike checking and savings accounts, which may have little to no balance requirements, Money Market Mutual Funds will often require a larger initial deposit (e.g., $2,000), but some may also allow no initial deposit as long as you "promise" to deposit a set amount for an established time period (e.g., $50 per month).

---

4   Money Market Mutual Funds differ from Money Market Funds. Please consult with your bank for particular details.

Essentially, a money market mutual fund is an investment vehicle that is usually managed by a team of experienced, financial professionals that we refer to as a *management team*. They may have a name for themselves such as the *Stable Value Fund* or they may simply call themselves the *Money Market Mutual Fund*. This team of professionals will accept deposits from investors. The thing is, there are usually hundreds of thousands, if not millions of investors depositing their monies with this money market mutual fund. The management team then pools all of the monies together, in one big pot, which usually represents a rather large sum of money (e.g., hundreds of millions or even billions) and then uses the big pot of pooled investor monies to invest in usually high-quality, short-term, liquid securities (i.e., cash investments). This may include securities such as certificates of deposit (CDs) and U.S. Treasury bills.[5] The money market mutual fund will then attempt to pay you monthly interest payments based on the underlying investments. On this note, you will not have direct ownership in the underlying investments. Instead, you own a proportional share of the overall pot of pooled investor monies. Make sense? Let's try to expand on this idea.

Money Market Mutual Funds attempt to have a cost of $1.00 per share. This means that if you invest $1,000 into a money market mutual fund, you should have 1,000 shares. It's a one-for-one calculation. For example, if at a later date you decide to withdraw $300, you will instruct the management team to liquidate 300 of your 1,000 shares. You will then be left with 700 shares in the pot, valued at $1 per share, for a total remaining amount of $700. Simple, right? Try not to overcomplicate it.

One important aspect of money market mutual funds is that they *attempt* to maintain a $1.00 per share value. This means that if you invest $1,000, your balance should not decrease (i.e., lose value) unless, of course, you withdraw some of your monies. Keep in mind though that the pooled pot of investor monies, which is commonly quite large, is usually spread out by the management team amongst a variety of cash equivalent investments. These underlying investments do have the potential to decline in value. If the value of the underlying investments

5   A Treasury bill (T-Bill) is a short-term debt obligation issued by the U.S. government.

declines, then the per-share value of the money market mutual fund may also decline. For example, perhaps a few of the underlying investments do not pan out as successfully as the management team had hoped and the per-share value of the fund is now calculated to be 95 cents. If this were to happen, then your $1,000 investment that initially netted you 1,000 shares will now be worth $950 (1,000 shares x .95 = $950). In this case, you have actually lost money. That's not to say that the value per share can't or won't go back up, the point is that you can lose money in a money market mutual fund. When the value of a money market drops below $1.00 per share, it is considered to have "broke the buck."

> **In the history of the money market, dating back to 1971, there was only one [money market mutual] fund that broke the buck until the 2008 financial crisis.**
>
> Yahoo! Finance

Once again, I'm not trying to be the bearer of bad news – doom and gloom –but it's important for you to understand the risks associated with various investments, and in this instance, money market mutual funds. Yes, they have the potential to decline in value, and as a result, you would end up losing money. However, money market mutual funds, historically, have not "broke the buck" very often. They have and they could again, but this is not typical. MMMFs are still classified as cash investments and fall within our cash bucket, which is the most conservative of the three buckets. As you will see later, bond and stock investments generally present much greater risk. It should be evident now that investors in a money market mutual fund are presented with substantially more risk, as small of a chance as it may be, when compared to other cash investments such as checking and savings accounts. As a result, you should expect to receive substantially larger monthly interest payments.

On a less dire note, Money Market Mutual Funds generally provide an investor with substantial liquidity. A money market mutual fund investor can usually initiate online funds transfers from the fund to an outside account, such as a checking account. However, from my experience, these types of electronic transfer of funds can take a few days to complete. In addition to the online funds transfer feature, a lot of Money Market Mutual Funds will provide an investor with check writing capabilities (i.e., a checkbook). However, there are usually stipulations such that a check can only be written for a minimum amount (for example, $250). So, even though money market mutual funds do provide liquidity, the liquidity of MMMFs generally lacks when compared to other cash investments such as checking accounts, which may allow on-demand access to your monies. For example, if you are perusing various garage sales on a Saturday morning and find that item you've always wanted, you will most likely not be using the funds in your MMMF at the direct point-of-sale.

We previously mentioned that money market mutual funds are run by a management team. The management team is expected, in part, to collect and pool investor monies, make investment choices (e.g., U.S. Treasury bills, CDs), continue to monitor those investments and make changes, issue checkbooks, provide ongoing account monitoring (e.g., customer statements), and a host of other responsibilities. All of these functions probably have costs associated with them, and as a result, you should expect that the management team will charge a fee so they can continue to provide these services as well as make a living themselves. Well, most money market mutual funds will assess this fee in the form of an *expense ratio*.

An expense ratio is essentially how the money market mutual fund management team makes money. This is not a fee that you directly pay in the sense that you will need to deposit monies or write a check to the management team. Rather, the expense ratio fee is generally deducted from the pooled pot of investor monies. You more than likely will never see the fee deduction, and it really shouldn't have too much of an impact on your investment. However, it is worth noting that you will pay this sort of fee in a money market mutual fund investment. Sure, fees suck, but the management team is providing a valuable service.

It should be evident at this point in our discussion that Money Market Mutual Funds, when compared to the other cash investments we have discussed (i.e., checking accounts, savings accounts, and CDs), require you to take on a much higher level of risk. As a result, you should expect to earn more interest when investing in a Money Market Mutual Fund, and the following table illustrates this point:

Table 1.2 - Interest Rates for the Years 2000, 2006 and 2016.

Investment	January 5, 2000	January 4, 2006	January 6, 2016
Checking Account	1.75	1.11	.01
Savings Account	2.01	1.91	.09
6-Month CD	4.63	2.84	.16
Money Market MF	5.07	4.89	1.01

Source: Bankrate.com

The above chart is the same one we presented earlier, but with the interest rates for Money Market Mutual Funds. Once again, when we look at the years 2000 and 2006, in some instances, money market mutual funds earned almost five times as much as other cash investments.

Cash Investments & Interest Payments

Ok, so we have spent the last few pages discussing four of the most common cash investments you'll run into throughout your investing life, but how might they benefit you, or not?

As we will see, there are other riskier assets within the bond and stock buckets whose primary goal is to grow your money, but that is simply not the case with cash investments. One of the most glaring characteristics of cash investments is that they are intended to preserve your money, which can be a good thing. For example, imagine that you have $5,000 saved away for your child's college tuition payment, which will be due in four months. Are you looking to potentially "gamble" that tuition payment in riskier investments, hoping that it will double in size, or are you mainly concerned with the $5,000 being there to cover your child's tuition payment? What if you've saved enough for a down payment on a new vehicle that you plan to purchase within the next few weeks? Once again, do you want to "gamble" that down payment in hopes of making money or do you want to ensure that the down payment will be covered? In these types of scenarios, cash investments may seem the most appropriate as their primary goal is to preserve what you have. However, not only will they attempt to preserve what you have, but most cash investments also pay interest, as modest as it may be.

Checking accounts, savings accounts, and money market mutual funds will generally pay interest on a monthly basis while certificates of deposit usually pay interest at the end of the maturity period. The timing of interest payments and the type of cash investment you choose can have a real effect on the quality of your financial life. For example, using the real-world interest rates from Table 1.2, if we invested $50,000 into a checking account in 2006 earning .01% interest we would expect to receive approximately $42 per month in interest.[6] However, if we assumed more risk and instead invested that same $50,000 in a Money Market Mutual Fund, we could expect around $203 per month in interest. This is a substantial difference and can drastically alter the quality of one's life. A retiree might use the $203 monthly interest payment as a sort of *supplemental income* to help pay bills or fund travel.

If you're not in retirement and don't need the monthly interest payments, you can reinvest those interest payments right back into your cash investment, which will ultimately lead to a steady growth of your balance. Plus, by leaving the interest payments in your account, that new, larger balance should generate an even higher interest payment going forward. Think of it as "interest on top of interest." This process is commonly referred to as *compound interest* and can be a highly beneficial investment technique. What you ultimately decide to do with your interest payments depends on your own personal situation and goals.

Harkening back to the introduction of this book, I stressed my strong desire that when you think of investments you remember the three buckets (cash, bonds, and stocks):

---

6   Calculated as a simple annualized interest rate: ($50,000 x 0.01)/12

The investments we have discussed up to this point can be classified as cash investments and as such, listed in our cash bucket.

Summary

We started off by discussing what can be considered one of the most basic investments – that of a checking account.

Checking accounts provide overall "safety" through features such as liquidity (e.g., debit cards, ATM withdrawals), government guarantee insurance (e.g., FDIC), and are usually very easy to open and maintain (e.g., low initial balance requirements). There just is not a lot of risk when it comes to checking accounts, and as a result, the return you will receive on a checking account should be expected to be very low.

Savings accounts were our next topic. We discussed how savings accounts can be harder for some of us to open and fund (larger initial investment amounts required) as well as providing us more risk through the lack of liquidity (e.g., lack of debit card and ATM withdrawals as well as higher check writing requirements). However, a savings account is usually still under the "protection" of FDIC insurance and can allow the transfer of funds to more liquid accounts (i.e., checking accounts). We then discussed perhaps some of the more risky of cash investments: Certificates of Deposit and Money Market Mutual Funds.

Certificates of Deposit present substantially more risk when compared to checking and savings accounts. CDs essentially "lock up" your money for a set amount of time – the *maturity* period. Any access to your money before the maturity period might require you to pay penalties and as a result, lose money. Also, CDs usually have set initial investment amounts that can be rather large for some investors. Yet still, CDs are usually under the auspices of FDIC insurance and have very little, if any, risk of losing your money so long as you hold onto the CD for the entire maturity period.

Money Market Mutual Funds are potentially the riskiest of the cash investments. After all, when investing in a MMMF you are "handing over" your money to a management team who will invest your money in various short-term, liquid cash type investments. These investments have the potential to lose value, and as a result, your MMMF could lose value (although this rarely happens). FDIC insurance does not apply to MMMFs so any loss in value would be the investors' to stomach. Also, since a MMMF is made up of a professional money management team, you can expect to pay fees for their services, usually in the form of an *expense ratio*. Although MMMFs can be regarded as the riskiest of the cash investments we have discussed, they do provide potential benefits. Often times, MMMFs will provide investors with liquidity usually in the form of check writing capabilities (albeit for minimum check writing amounts such as $250) and electronic transfer of funds to more liquid accounts (including the wiring of funds).

All in all, cash investments are the most conservative of investments often times providing us liquidity, government insurance, and very little, if any, risk. The old adage still holds true: the greater the risk, the greater the expected return. As a result, cash investments will provide us the lowest of investment returns. The below illustration summarizes for you the various investments within the cash bucket. Hopefully, this illustration will help you to easily recall what investments are considered cash investments.

So, now that we have covered the first of three buckets, what about the other two?

Chapter 3

The Bond Bucket

In order to practice the career I'm in, I've had to obtain various federal and state licenses. Fresh out of college and new to the investment industry, I began to study for my first one. I clearly remember that the topic of bonds presented some rather challenging, rather dry material with in-depth discussions on characteristics such as *maturity, yield, discount, interest rates,* and the like. Often, I'd see brokers yawning with one hand propping up their head and their glasses sitting on the table while others were asleep with their arms crossed and their head on the table. In all honestly, bond discussions have this affect.

However, over the course of my professional career, I have realized that bonds can play a critical role in an investment portfolio, and it is worth having a discussion about. So, if you must, feel free to place your glasses on the table, perhaps grab a small pillow and fill up your coffee as we journey together through the topic of bonds!

In the previous chapter, we discussed cash investments. We looked at how there are quite a few different forms of cash investments within the cash bucket. Some of these investments pose more risk (and as a result, hopefully more return) than others. For example, Money Market Mutual Funds may lose value, or your investment in a Certificate of Deposit may be inaccessible to you during the maturity period. However, even though there are these varying levels of risk among cash investments, they are all still part of the most conservative investment class we can invest in: cash.

Bonds, on the other hand, are a definite step up in risk. But just like cash investments, there are different types of bonds with different types of risk and potential returns. I will attempt to start off by introducing you to some very basic bond discussions and then gradually introduce more complex topics such as the risks associated with bond investing. By the end of this chapter we will be able to fill up the empty bond bucket, just like we did with the cash bucket, and hopefully, this investing thing will start to make a little more sense to you.

Mortgages and Bonds

Many of us are familiar with the basics of how a mortgage works and so I always like to first discuss the basics of a mortgage transaction and then relate this familiar transaction to that of a bond investment.

For a good portion of society, purchasing a home is one of the biggest expenses of our lifetime. I imagine that many of us, unless we are fortunate enough to be independently wealthy or a financial windfall has befallen us, do not have the cash on hand to purchase a home outright. Instead, we will rely on obtaining a mortgage loan through a financial institution, usually a bank. By lending you their money (through a mortgage loan), the financial institution is essentially making an investment in you. In the next few pages we will reference a mortgage transaction with the following features: a 25-year mortgage with a principal loan amount of $200,000.

This means that over the course of 25 years we will be expected to payback a portion of the original loan amount (usually in monthly installments) such that at the end of the 25 years the lender will have recouped their entire $200,000 investment. But is it that simple? After all, the lender could be investing their money in potentially other more lucrative investments. Also, how certain can the lender be that you will actually honor your monthly principal repayments (i.e., monthly mortgage payments)? What happens if you can't afford to make the payments? Are there some of us who are more prone to miss payments?

Remember from our cash discussion that, as investors, if we take on more risk (more uncertainty), we will demand a higher rate of return. This same concept holds true for lenders who are essentially the investor in our mortgage example. With that said, given the multitude of risks they are taking on by lending us money, they will require a commensurate return, and this return is manifested in the form of interest payments that are charged as part of the loan. But what are some of these risks? Well, let's start to discuss some of them and, as we will see later, bond investors will face many of the same risks.

Default Risk

One of the main risks faced by mortgage lenders is that of default risk or the idea that the individual(s) they lent money to will be unable to make the required monthly mortgage payments. For example, some mortgagees may not have a job with sufficient income to make their monthly payments. Others may have a history of lengthy unemployment and this could indicate the potential for future missed mortgage payments.

DEFAULT RISK: THE CHANCE THAT COMPANIES OR INDIVIDUALS WILL BE UNABLE TO MAKE THE REQUIRED PAYMENTS ON THEIR DEBT OBLIGATIONS.

Perhaps there are mortgagees who have amassed large amounts of debt which, when coupled with a mortgage payment, could indicate a lack of adequate income and as a result, the potential to miss future mortgage payments.

On the flipside, there may be mortgagees who have solid work histories and little to no outstanding debt, who have consistently paid off their debts. Also, those with solid work histories with short (or non-existent) times of unemployment. It would make sense then that riskier mortgagees would be charged a higher interest rate given that the lender is taking on additional risk. It may seem "unfair," but let's remember that the lender is an investor and just like us, when we take on more risk, we should expect the potential for higher reward.

With the onset of the 2008/2009 mortgage crisis, we witnessed the jobless rate in the U.S. economy jump to levels not seen in decades. As more and more people lost their jobs (and subsequent income), they could no longer make payments on their mortgages and as a result, many financial institutions that issued mortgages, were not receiving their promised monthly payments. Sometimes, these types of scenarios are temporary and eventually the individual will once again be able to make the monthly mortgage payments, but other times they cannot.

Another, perhaps even greater, risk to the lender is that of a foreclosure, in which case the lender may not receive the entirety of their $200,000 "investment." In fact, in the case of a foreclosure, the lender may be forced to receive only pennies on the dollar. This is because a foreclosure usually means a mortgagee will no longer be able to make the *promised* mortgage payments, usually just *walking away* from the loan, and as a result, the lender will not recoup its investment.

In 2009, "a record 2.8 million properties with a mortgage got a foreclosure notice…jumping 21 percent from 2008 and 120 percent from 2007…"[7] The risk of default is a very real risk.

Opportunity Risk

Another risk posed to lenders, and this should be a rather simple idea to understand, is *opportunity risk*. Yes, lenders are in the business of lending monies, but they give up opportunities to invest money when they lend it out. So, when they lend you $200,000 for 25 years, they are not able to use that $200,000 to capitalize on potentially better investment opportunities. Perhaps the bank could use the same $200,000 to issue a small business loan to a promising company, but they can't because the money is tied up in your mortgage. And frankly, maybe the bank chooses not to make loans and instead holds onto its money.

---

7   Lynn Adler, U.S. 2009 foreclosures shatter record despite aid, http://www.reuters.com/article/us-usa-housing-foreclosures-idUSTRE60D0LZ20100114

Interest Rate Risk

The concept of interest rate risk may sometimes seem complex, but let's try to make sense of it. We will attempt to do this through a basic discussion of economics.

I imagine it would be no surprise to us that our US economy ebbs and flows. The US economy has periods in which it is roaring along (what we will call an *expansion* phase) and periods in which the economy is barely chugging along (what we will call a *contraction* phase). I like to relate our economy to that of a car engine. If we cruise along at 100 mph for too long, our engine could overheat and lead to a breakdown requiring us to pull over to the side of the road and give our engine time to cool down. On the contrary, if we are traveling too slowly, we may not get to our destination as quickly as we could and we are not utilizing the most of our car's output. Finding this balance is essentially the root of economic policies and often times can be more of an art than a science – there usually aren't perfect and clear answers.

This sort of economic research, analysis, and subsequent policy decisions is the foundation of the Federal Reserve Board (FRB or "The Fed"). The FRB was created by Congress to provide the nation with a safer, more flexible, and more stable monetary and financial system. It is the responsibility of The Fed to ensure our economy is not overheating nor being underutilized (to use the car analogy) and the Fed accomplishes this mainly through interest rate policy.

Interest rates in the United States are essentially established by the Federal Reserve Board. The rates set by the FRB, through the *discount rate*, have a trickle-down effect on interest rates in the overall economy. Everything from checking accounts to housing and car loans to the issuance of new bonds are all affected by the discount rate set by the FRB.

Financial institutions usually set their interest rates based on what the discount rate is currently at. If the Fed raises the *discount rate*, we can expect consumer loans (e.g., mortgages, new car loans, personal loans, small business loans) to also have increasing rates tied to them. Additionally, certain interest bearing accounts such as checking accounts should also start to increase the interest rates they pay out to customers. So, it's not all bad.

If a financial institution has lent you $200,000 and is charging you 7% interest, yet in a few years, interest rates in the economy increase to 9%, they are missing out on potentially higher interest payments. However, the financial institution could also benefit if, for example, they charge you 7%, but future interest rates decrease to 4%. This is the basic idea behind interest rate risk, that you could potentially miss out on higher interest payments. This basic tenant, as we will discuss shortly, holds true for bond investing. But bond investing has another added element rather than simply missing out on potentially higher interest rates: the element of bond prices (i.e., the value of your bond investment) increasing or decreasing in value with interest rate movements.

With these risks in mind (i.e., *default risk, opportunity risk,* and *interest rate risk*), let us turn our attention to bond investing.

Bonds

Bonds are typically issued by either governments (city, state, and federal) or corporations and are usually issued in minimum investment denominations of $1,000 all the way up to millions of dollars. Governments and corporations will usually issue bonds for expensive undertakings. For example, if a corporation wants to build a new manufacturing plant or office building, this project could cost hundreds of millions of dollars, if not more. Being such a large sum of money, a corporation may not have the cash on hand to cover all of the costs and will most likely need to "finance" this new project. This would be very similar to us not having enough money to purchase a house outright and instead seek out a mortgage loan. Well, one option corporations have to raise the required *capital* (i.e., money) would be to issue bonds. Let's try to explain just what a bond is.

When thinking of bond investments I want you to recall a simple mortgage transaction with the exception that the bond investor (you) is the lender and the corporation issuing the bond is the one seeking financing from you. Even though you are the one providing financing for the corporation (by investing in their bond), you do not set the terms of the bond, the corporation does. The good news though is that there can be as many bond terms as there are corporations (e.g., different maturities, interest rates). For our purposes, let us use the example of a corporation issuing a bond with a 15-year maturity, a 7% semi-annual interest payment, and a minimum investment amount of $1,000. But what does all of that mean (e.g., 15 year this, 7% that, semi-annual this)?

Well, for starters let's think back to the mortgage transaction I explained earlier. When investing in bonds you are essentially entering into a transaction similar to a mortgage, with an exception being that the roles are reversed and you are now the lender. The corporation is coming to you, the investor, to raise capital. The corporation is asking that you provide them $1,000 and they "promise" that in 15 years they will return to you your original investment (i.e., your $1,000 investment). This means you will receive the 7% semi-annual interest payment, but not recover your initial investment until the 15 year maturity has been reached. Could you potentially access your invested money before maturity? Yes, but you would likely suffer losses – more on this later. In addition, as we will discuss shortly, the corporation understands that you will be taking on risks (e.g., opportunity risk, default risk, and interest rate risk) so they will need to offer you a commensurate return, or with bond investing what we will refer to as interest.

So, over the course of those 15 years, the corporation will make two interest payments to you per year (i.e., semi-annual) based on an interest rate of 7%. We calculate the amount of this interest payment by multiplying your invested amount ($1,000) by the interest rate (7% or .07) to arrive at a figure of $70. However, this figure represents the annual interest. Since we will be paid twice a year, we divide the annual interest ($70) by 2 to arrive at a $35 interest payment every six months (i.e., semi-annual). Easy enough, right?

Now it should be mentioned that some of us might think $35 every six months is not that attractive of an interest payment, but keep in mind we are basing our calculations on a $1,000 investment. With larger investment amounts, that interest payment could increase substantially.

Let's assume our initial investment was $50,000 instead of $1,000. The semi-annual interest payment would then increase to $1,750.[8]

The above discussion lays out for you the basics of a bond investment. You invest your money with a corporation who promises to pay back your initial invested amount in the future at a set date (i.e., the *maturity*). In addition, over the course of the maturity period, the corporation will make interest payments to you (in our example, every six months or put another way, semi-annually). But what are some risks that you face when investing in a bond? Think back to our mortgage example.

One of the risks associated with bond investing is what we referred to as *opportunity risk* or the idea that you will miss out on other, potentially more beneficial, investment opportunities. In essence, the money you invest in a bond is "tied up" for the maturity period. In our previous example, the maturity period is 15 years. That is quite a long time to have your money tied up in an investment. Perhaps during those 15 years a more appealing investment is available to you. Well, you would potentially miss out on that opportunity because your money is in a 15-year bond. So, just like the bank who lent you $200,000 for a home loan, we too (in a bond investment) may miss other more lucrative investment options (opportunity risk).

Another risk posed by investing in bonds is *default risk*. Once again, I would like you to think back to our previous mortgage example. We discussed how some lendees may pose greater risk over others (e.g., questionable employment history, large amounts of debt). Well, corporations, like individuals, are fallible. Some corporations may have a track record of managing their financial affairs with great results. Perhaps these types of corporations have issued debt in the past and made all promised payments to investors. Yet, there may be corporations who have a rockier past when it comes to their financial affairs. Perhaps these corporations have missed bond payments in the past or, worse yet, they could be on the verge of bankruptcy, which means that the company may not be able to pay back the debt they

---

8   The calculation is as follows: $50,000 x .07 = $3,500 annual interest. $3,500 divided by 2 equals a semi-annual interest payment of $1,750.

owe you. Since bonds do not receive any sort of backing (e.g., FDIC insurance), you will essentially have to "eat the loss."[9] These are very real risks that you as an investor need to consider when investing in bonds.

Interest Rate Risk

Another risk as it relates to bond investing that I would like to bring to your attention is that of *interest rate risk*. Simply put, interest rate risk means that you could potentially receive a higher interest rate (i.e., make more money) at a later date. Perhaps you are invested in a 15-year bond that pays 7%, but in year five, newer issued bonds are paying 9% interest. You still have ten years left before your current bond matures and hence, will miss out on the higher paying bonds. This should be a rather simple concept to grasp, however, there is a larger underlying risk within this mix. Let's briefly discuss this important aspect of bond investing continuing with our previous bond example.

Assuming you purchased a $10,000, 15-year corporate bond that pays 7% interest semi-annually. This means that you have invested $10,000, which you will expect to receive back in 15 years, but that during those fifteen years you will receive interest payments of $350 every six months. What happens if, for example, in year three you run into an emergency and need access to the money? Can you perhaps sell the bond?

INTEREST RATE RISK: THE RISK THAT AN INVESTMENT'S VALUE (E.G., BONDS) WILL CHANGE DUE TO A CHANGE IN THE ABSOLUTE LEVEL OF INTEREST RATES

The technical answer is yes, you may be able to sell your bond before the maturity period, but there are potential hazards associated with this. For example, let's assume that in year three a newer $10,000, 15-year corporate bond is now paying 9% interest semi-annual. This means that a newer investor (whom you will want to sell your bond to) has the choice between investing in your bond or the newer issued bond. In essence, the new investor can choose between investing $10,000 by

---

9   In the event of bankruptcy and/or liquidation, bond holders do have a "place in line" when it comes to the distribution of assets to creditors. However, there is no guarantee that you will receive your invested money back.

buying your bond and receive $350 every six months or invest $10,000 on a newer bond and receive $450 every six months. The choice might be obvious, but not so fast!

So, how could you entice this newer investor to purchase your lower yielding bond? In order to attract an investor to purchase your bond, which is yielding less than the newer bonds, you may need to consider selling your bond at a *discount*. What does selling your bond at a *discount* mean?

Perhaps you will sell your bond for $8,000. Remember, you initially invested $10,000 and now are potentially selling it for $8,000 (a discount). If the investor took your offer, they would then have invested $8,000 in a bond that will pay them 7% semi-annually (the lower interest rate amount), and at the end of the 15-year maturity they will receive $10,000. In this example, the investor is receiving the lower semi-annual interest payments, but they will also receive $10,000 at the maturity date even though they only invested $8,000. The investor has made a capital gain of $2,000.

Essentially, this $2,000 capital gain is what enticed this investor to accept lower interest payments semi-annually. In this example, the good news is that you were able to access your money by selling your bond, but the bad news is that you suffered a $2,000 loss. Remember, you initially invested $10,000 and just sold it for $8,000. When you sell a bond for less then what it is worth, that is considered selling a bond at a *discount*.

The opposite can also be true. Using the same example, let's assume you decide to sell your bond, but this time, newer similar bonds are yielding 4%. This means that your bond is paying more interest semi-annually than newer-issue bonds. An investor may find your 7% semi-annual interest payments more attractive than similar bonds yielding only 4%. If the investor wants your 7% bond, you will probably consider selling your bond at a *premium*.

BOND PREMIUM: A BOND TRADES AT A PREMIUM WHEN IT OFFERS A COUPON RATE HIGHER THAN PREVAILING INTEREST RATES.

You essentially hold the upper hand in this instance. Perhaps you sell your bond for $11,750. In this case, you have made a "*gain*" on your money, whereas the newer investor is essentially losing $1,750 because they are paying $11,750 for a bond that after the 15 year maturity will return to them $10,000. The newer investor may be willing to take this "loss" because they will receive higher interest payments every six months, when compared to the newer, lower yielding bonds.

Hopefully, the above examples have provided you some insight into interest rate risk at it relates to bond investing. There is a rather simple saying that can sum up all that we discussed about interest rate risk and bonds and that is that as interest rates go up, bond prices go down. This can further be illustrated using an illustration of a teeter-totter:

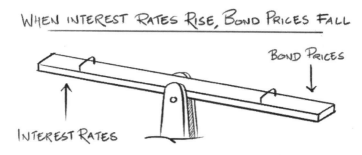

We just spent a few pages discussing how bond investing can be related to a simple mortgage transaction. We also discussed some main risks associated with bond investing (i.e., *opportunity risk*, *default risk*, and *interest rate risk*). At this point, it will be beneficial to discuss the two types of issuers of bonds: corporations and governments.

Corporate and Government Bonds

Bonds are issued by either corporations or government entities. When we discussed how a mortgage loan is granted to a mortgagee, I explained that some mortgagees may have a history of bad debt management or job history that could indicate the potential for future missed mortgage payments (i.e., *default risk*). These types of risks will most likely dictate higher interest rate charges for these individuals. The same concept can be attributed to bonds.

Government bonds, which in essence act the same way as the corporate bonds we have been discussing, are generally considered the most conservative of bond investments. This is due, in part, to the fact that the US Federal Government is considered the safest lender in the world. This means that if you loan money to the US Government (e.g., in the form of a bond investment), you can expect to receive your interest payments on time and your principal invested amount at the end of the maturity period. In fact, with government issued bonds your payments (of both principal and interest) can be considered guaranteed. The word "guaranteed" is a huge no-no in the world of investing. Guaranteeing something, particularly when it comes to finances, can open a world of hurt. However, with government issued securities we can say that the investment is essentially guaranteed.

One of the main reasons for this assurance is that the US Government has taxing authority and in theory can always raise taxes should the nation's coffers run low. In essence, the government (both federal and state/local) can simply raise taxes to ensure debts (i.e., bond principal and interest payments) are met. It would be a dire day if the US Government had to default on its interest payments or not make principal repayments at maturity.

Corporations, on the other hand, do not have the authority to tax. The interest payments "promised" by a corporation are on shakier ground and will be dependent on how well the corporation manages its financial house. But still, some corporations may have a more promising track record than others. Corporations that have a track record of being more timely lendees and that are viewed by the public at large as "safer," may not have to pay as much interest to their investors given the appearance of added safety. Conversely, riskier bond issuers would generally be required to make higher interest payments to bond investors.

An important distinction needs to be drawn between bonds issued by the U.S. federal government and bonds issued by states, cities, and localities.

Municipal Bonds

When bonds are issued by the federal government, we refer to them simply as *bonds* or *government bonds*. However, when bonds are issued by state, city, or local municipalities, we refer to them as *municipal bonds*. This is in an important distinction and one that you will want to be aware of as you venture into the investing world.

First, municipal bonds are just that: bonds. We do not need to complicate it any more than that. They are issued with various maturity periods with stated interest rate payments. However, unlike government bonds, municipal bonds have a particular feature concerning the taxation (or lack thereof) of municipal bond interest payments. On this note, we will cover the basics of investment taxation in Chapter 8, so we will save a more in-depth discussion of taxation for then, but it would be appropriate to touch on the basics of taxation now as it relates to municipal bond interest payments.

When we receive bond interest payments above a certain amount (e.g., $10), we will most likely owe income tax on those interest payments. At the end of the year, we will receive a statement that shows how much interest we received. We then use that statement to report to the IRS and, subsequently, pay any mandatory taxes. The taxation of interest received on bonds is usually assessed at the federal level, but (depending on the state you live in) also on a state and/or local level. This taxation of bond interest is usually assessed on interest paid by federal government bonds as well as corporate bonds. However, municipal bond interest payments can be exempt from federal taxation and, in some instances, state and local taxes. But why might this be?

Municipal bonds are usually issued to assist a locality in engaging in improvements that may help the overall community. For example, a municipal bond might be issued to build a new water treatment facility or upgrade the local sewer system. There is a slew of reasons why a municipality might issue bonds, but they usually have the effect of benefiting the community at large. To incentivize investors to invest in their own communities, which might also save the federal government from having to dole out money for these communities, the IRS provides a tax-exempt status to the interest received on municipal bonds. As always, there is a catch and that *catch* is the Alternative Minimum Tax or what is commonly referred to as the *AMT Tax*.

For a majority of us, we will be able to take advantage of the tax-exempt status of municipal bond interest, but there are limitations for the wealthiest of investors. Essentially, the IRS will disallow the tax-exempt features of municipal bond interest for those individuals classified as wealthy. What does this mean? The IRS sets limits as to what amount of income and/or net worth classifies an individual as wealthy. Regardless of what these limits are, just know that for those considered wealthy, although they can still invest in municipal bonds, they may have to pay taxes on the interest received through municipal bonds.

The overriding point for you to remember is that municipal bonds act like any *normal* bond (e.g., corporate or government bonds) with the exception that the interest received on municipal bonds might be exempt from taxation at the federal and/or state and local levels.

On this note, there are numerous ratings agencies whose job it is to analyze the various issuers of bonds and assign them a ratings score, which will help investors determine which bond issuers pose the least (or most) amount of risk.

Ratings

It is probably evident, and most of us have probably experienced, that when we obtain loans (e.g., personal, auto, home) the lender will run a credit check on us. This credit check is usually represented with a credit score. Our scores are then compared to other individuals seeking loans, and we are essentially ranked based on our risk level. That is, those with lower credit scores are considered riskier and as such, will probably be charged a higher interest rate for a loan.

When it comes to bond investing we rank corporations in a similar matter. This allows us, the investors, to determine the riskiness of each bond issuer. If a certain bond issuer is considered riskier, then we as investors should expect a higher interest rate when compared to less risky issuers. There are three main companies who specialize in providing ratings on bonds: Moody's®, Standard & Poor's®, and Fitch®.

Unlike credit reports, which provide us a rating in the form of a number (e.g., 650), the above rating agencies label the ratings of bonds with numbers (e.g., Aaa, BBB). Let's briefly look at the rating system for these agencies keeping in mind that the ratings relate to how risky a particular bond is.

Table 2.3(a) - Bond Rating Agencies – Investment Grade

Moody's®	Standard & Poor's®	Fitch Ratings®
Aaa	AAA	AAA
Aa	AA	AA
A	A	A
Baa	BBB	BBB
Ba	BB	BB
B	B	B

Source: Moody's®, Fitch®, and S&P®

Table 2.3(b) – Bond Rating Agencies – Non-Investment Grade or "Junk Bonds"

Moody's®	Standard & Poor's®	Fitch Ratings®
Caa	CCC	CCC
Ca	CC	CC
C	D	D

Source: Moody's®, Fitch®, and S&P®

Bonds with ratings B and above (for all three major ratings agencies) are considered investment grade (Table 2.3(a)). Those below B are considered non-investment grade or *"junk"* bonds (Table 2.3(b)). The above tables may seem chaotic. It's not necessary to remember all of the various letters and what they mean. Rather, what I want you to remember is that we classify bonds as either investment grade or non-investment grade.

Investment-Grade Bonds

Investment-grade bonds are considered the least risky for investors. Granted, as we learned in prior chapters, bonds inherently hold risk (e.g., interest rate risk), but investment-grade bonds are the "safer" option. Think of our loan example and having a credit score assigned to us. Investment-grade bonds would be those of us with the highest credit scores. These ratings do not suggest a guarantee that these higher quality bonds will pan out over time, but that the companies issuing these types of bonds have demonstrated the capability and capacity to meet their debt obligations As a result, these companies will not be forced to offer higher interest payments on their bond issues. For you as an investor, this may or may not be good news. First, by investing in investment-grade bonds you may receive lower interest payments (when compared to non-investment grade bonds, which we will cover momentarily), but the flip side is you are investing in a bond that has a high probability of paying you interest in full and on time as well as returning your invested amount at maturity.

Non-Investment Grade "Junk Bonds"

Junk bonds, or non-investment grade bonds, are the riskiest bond investments. Generally, these are bonds issued by corporations who have usually experienced or are experiencing rather dire financial circumstances. Essentially, these companies are more prone to miss interest payments, repayment of principal or even default on their bonds all together. That's not to say these companies won't "right the ship," but they definitely pose a greater risk to investors. Once again we are reminded of the old adage, *the greater the risk, the greater the expected return*. As a result, non-investment grade companies are forced to provide higher-yielding bonds in order to attract investors.

I feel it's necessary to reinforce the notion that "junk" bonds pose great amounts of risk and you should tread lightly in investing in these types of bonds. You see, during the course of my career I have witnessed periods of economic growth and economic downturns, times in which interest rates were increasing and times when interest rates were decreasing. In fact, since the Great Recession, interest rates have been at historically low levels for an extended period of time—almost a decade.

During periods of decreasing interest rates, investors often *"chase yields."* What does *"chasing yields"* look like? Well, during times of high interest rates, bond investors are often elated with the substantial interest payments, but in times of low interest rates are shocked at the seemingly miniscule amount of interest being paid. In an attempt to obtain higher interest payments, bond investors may start to consider investing in "junk" bonds because (as we have just discussed) they will usually offer substantially higher interest payments. Remember though that these companies are usually forced to offer these higher interest payments because of their *"rocky"* financial footing. This is what we call *"chasing yields"* or *"yield chasing."* This is a pattern of investing that you will want to avoid. That is not to say that you should avoid junk bonds all together, but they should be a very limited portion of your overall bond investment portfolio.

Opportunity Risk

Another risk when investing in bonds is that of *opportunity risk*, which can refer to maturity period (or how long your investment is "locked up"). In our previous corporate bond example, we assumed a 15-year maturity period. Again, this entails that for 15 years your investment will be tied up in a bond. To some of us, that is a long time to tie up your money. Well, bond maturities can vary greatly. Bonds, both Government and corporate, can be issued from one year to as far out as a few decades. Typically speaking, bonds that are issued with less than two-year maturities are considered *short-term* bonds, those with maturities ranging from two to five years can be considered *intermediate-term* bonds, and those bonds with maturities of great than five years are considered *long-term* bonds. The shorter amount of time your money is tied up (i.e., the lower the maturity), the less risk you are assuming and as a result, the less return you can expect.

What this tells us is that while we are invested in a bond, during the maturity period, interest rates will more than likely fluctuate and, as a result, your bond value will decrease or increase. This is a basic concept of bond investing: as interest rates increase, bond prices decrease and as interest rates decrease, bond prices increase (remember the teeter-totter). However, so long as you hold onto your bond until it matures, you can expect to receive back your initial investment regardless of the price fluctuations in the market. Allow me to share with you an experience I had with one of my clients that will hopefully put into perspective the importance of understanding this fundamental characteristic of bonds.

It was the mid-2000s when interest rates in the overall economy were gradually increasing. At the time, I was working with high net worth clients and one in particular still stands out in my mind. She was a widow in her 80s and her husband had recently passed. Over the course of her marriage, her husband had taken care of their finances and now that he had passed, their investments overwhelmed her. In particular, an investment of approximately $1 million dollars in a bond mutual fund.[10] All she really knew about this particular bond investment was that it would send her monthly interest payments. Given the size of their investment, these interest payments were quite substantial and provided her a source of retirement income.

We met because she was absolutely terrified at her recent account statement showing a rather dramatic decrease in the principal value of their bond investment. Whereas they initially invested close to $1 million dollars, the investment was now valued at around $895,000. Understandably she was quite shaken, particularly given that her husband was no longer around to watch over their investments. When I asked her what she knew about bond investing, her response was something similar to, "I don't know, other than I receive interest payments from this bond that I use for spending money."

I then proceeded to explain some of the basic concepts surrounding bonds – just like we have done in the preceding pages. That is, we discussed how as interest rates in the economy increase, bond prices typically decrease. At that time, interest rates were in fact increasing and this was one of the main reasons behind the drop in their bond investment value. I asked if she anticipated needing access to the bond investment prior to its maturity and she emphatically stated that she would not. In fact, she really liked the interest payments the bond investment was producing for her. Well, guess what? Since she didn't

---

10   Chapter 6 discusses mutual funds.

anticipate needing the bond investment prior to maturity, should could just "let it ride" and when interest rates eventually decrease, her bond value will go up. In the meantime, since interest rates have increased, she would be receiving a larger periodic interest payment. It was her new-found knowledge regarding the basic relationship between interest rates and bond prices that relieved her anxiety. Sure, bond prices and interest rates act inversely, but as long as she holds onto her bond until maturity, she will expect to receive back the entire amount invested and, over the course of the maturity period, enjoy the interest payments, which is exactly the course she was on and decided to stay on—no drastic measures were required.

We have spent quite a few pages digesting a lot of information surrounding bonds, albeit at a basic level. Even though we have kept our information at a basic level, some of you might still feel overwhelmed and understandably so. Many of us in the finance profession sometimes find the volume of information we deal with to be overwhelming. I have found that a good way to keep things simple is through illustrations. One of the first illustrations I would like to present to you is a three-by-three grid. Quite frequently, financial articles will reference this same grid so it might benefit you to be exposed to it.

BONDS

CORPORATE	BLEND	GOVERNMENT	
			LONG-TERM
			INTERMEDIATE -TERM
			SHORT-TERM

Think of each cell in the grid as one of the various types of bond investments. As discussed in prior chapters, there are two main issuers of bonds: corporations and government entities (columns). By now you should know that corporate bonds are typically riskier than government bonds. In addition to classifying bonds as either corporate or government, we classify bonds based on their maturity. Bond maturities are either short-, intermediate-, or long-term. To keep it simple, think of it that the longer your money is "locked up," the more risk you are assuming. That is to say, longer-term bonds generally pose more risk compared to their short-term counterparts. I would also like to introduce to you now, although we will cover this more in the chapter on mutual funds, to the concept of a blended bond. Again, this has to do with mutual funds, but essentially indicates a bond investment that incorporates both corporate and government bonds – hence, a blend.

Summary

At the beginning of this chapter we briefly touched on the topic of a simple mortgage transaction. I am certain many of you have this basic knowledge, and it is this basic knowledge of a mortgage transaction that can help us understand bond investing.

A bond investment is essentially where you act as a lender to a corporation or government entity. The typical stipulations of the investment are a maturity period and interest rate. The maturity is the length of time the corporation will use your money, after which, they will repay your original invested amount. These maturity periods can vary greatly ranging anywhere from one year up to decades. During this maturity period, the corporation will pay you interest usually every six months (semi-annual).[11] Often times, retirees will invest in bonds and use the higher interest payments (when compared to cash investments) as supplemental income. Using our examples from earlier, a $50,000 investment in a checking account might produce $300 every six months whereas a $50,000 investment in a bond could produce

---

11 The typical bond interest payment is paid out in semi-annual (twice a year) payments, but not all bonds have the same interest payment schedule. When researching a bond pay attention to its interest payment schedule.

$1,750 every six months. This larger interest payment might seem attractive, but keep in mind there are added risks in bond investing when compared to cash investments.

Some of the most prominent risks of bond investing are *default risk*, *opportunity risk*, and *interest rate risk*. It is these risks that will dictate a higher interest rate payment than you would see with cash investments.

Now that we have covered some of the basics of bond investing, I would like to present to you an illustration that encapsulates all of the bond investments we have discussed. At the beginning of the chapter our bond bucket was empty. Now we can start to fill it up, and hopefully this investing thing is now starting to make a little more sense:

Chapter 4

The Stock Bucket

From my almost twenty years' experience in brokerage firms, I know that stocks present a bag of mixed emotions for most of us. The general consensus seems to be that stocks are where fortunes are made and lost; that stocks and the stock market conjure up grandiose images of riches and power. At the same time, stocks are confusing and complex – an investment playground for elites and the wealthy. Well, the first part is true. You absolutely could lose your entire investment in stocks, but you also stand to gain a great deal. As for complexity, I can certainly understand where that idea comes from, but I am here to help you make sense of it all.

Clients usually came to me inquiring about investing in stocks, not really knowing what stocks were about except that they expected stocks to provide them substantial investment gains. They would usually regal successful, yet usually abnormal, stories surrounding investment gains that a friend or relative made by investing in a particular stock and that they would like to mirror those gains. When we get down to it, I would often times tell them to forget what they heard from their friend or relative and for us to start down the road of understanding the basics first.

A frightening idea I hear from people, that sends a shiver down my spine, is when they enthusiastically tell me that a friend, work colleague, or even family member has discussed with them a particular stock ,and they want to invest money in that stock. When I inquire with them a bit deeper about what they were told or what they know about this stock, it usually seems to mimic a game of telephone. It starts off with a friend who heard from a guy that spoke with a woman that works at the company who heard from a television program that this stock is going to increase in value.

On one hand, who's to say this information may not lead to an investment that could make you rich? Maybe it will. But on the other hand, maybe it won't. In my opinion, this is an extremely inappropriate way to approach investing in stocks. So, what is the best way to invest in stocks? Well, let's start with the basics.

Introduction to Stocks

In Chapter 3, we looked at bonds and how they work. When it comes to issuing those bonds, I told you that corporations will often issue bonds to help them finance very expensive projects such as new manufacturing plants or other capital intensive infrastructure. A lot of corporations may not have $200 million dollars in cash to finance these projects, so they raise those funds by issuing bonds. Well, another form of financing that a company can use to raise capital is through issuing stocks.

When a company issues stocks, they are essentially obtaining financing from investors. When you buy stocks, you invest in a company by providing them money. In turn, the company provides you with a stock certificate, which is basically an IOU. In days past, this IOU was in the form of an actual stock certificate – a piece of paper with the companies name, logo, amount of shares you actually bought, and the like. It should be noted that in modern times, stock certificates, such as *The Walt Disney* example below, are no longer issued in physical form and instead are recorded electronically.

Example of a stock certificate – *The Walt Disney Company*

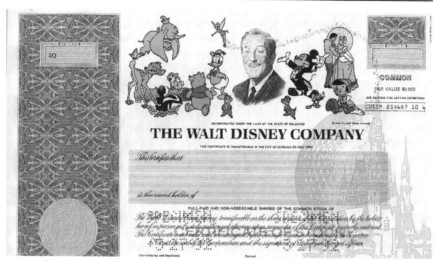

It is assumed that at any time you may go back to the company (or financial markets) and "turn in" your IOU to receive your money back. The thing is, the value of the stock certificate (the IOU) can change based on many factors outside of your control and may be worth more or less then what you originally paid for it. Generally speaking, the value will be based on how well the company you have invested in manages their business. Do they have a product that many people will purchase and not only purchase once, but on an ongoing basis? Will the company be able to manage their financial affairs in a satisfactory manner (e.g., no account scandals, appropriate budgets to weather economic storms)? There are many variables that can affect the price of a stock and those will ultimately determine the value of your investment.

Remember that certain investments, such as bonds, may have an initial base value of $1,000. Although the value of the bond will fluctuate with the market, the payout of that bond will always be $1,000 at maturity. This is not the case with stocks. Individual stock prices can vary greatly ranging anywhere from a few pennies per share to hundreds of thousands of dollars and, in theory, we can purchase a minimum of one share of a company. So, if a stock is trading at $10 per share, you could theoretically invest in this company's stock with only $10. Another stock might be priced at $350 per share, so your minimum investment would be $350.[12]

But, why is it that some stocks may require only pennies for an initial investment while other stocks may require a much larger initial investment? That's the first topic I want to cover.

Stock Prices

I want you to imagine that you own and run a lemonade stand. Part of your lemonade business is a portable lemonade stand that you tow to different spots in the city. You tow it downtown during lunch hour and then in front of sporting venues when they have games.

Perhaps your stand is made of metal with charming wood accents intertwined throughout. Inside, you have a cooler or two that holds ice and fresh lemons and a lemonade mixing machine and a portable generator to keep everything running. And of course, you have a vehicle that you use to tow the stand around town.

Let's assume that your lemonade is a hit. The downtown lunchtime crowds line up to get a taste of your lemonade and sports fans do the same. You believe that if you could improve a few things, your business could flourish and you could make more money. So you decide that you want to expand your business.

One of your first moves might be to upgrade your stand to a larger and more modern one with signage to list your various products and awnings to provide shade to your customers. You have also been eyeing a new mixing machine that will make lemonade at a faster rate, which will allow you to meet a higher demand. You might even decide to upgrade your generator and, in an attempt to save money, trade-in and upgrade your vehicle to a more fuel efficient one.

---

12 There are a variety of potential costs (e.g., commissions) that may make purchasing one share of stock not feasible. We will cover more of these costs in Chapter 12. For now, let's stick to the basics.

These ambitious business improvements may certainly help your business grow and succeed, but they also probably require an outlay of cash. At this point, you would need to assess whether or not you have enough savings to cover these costs (and even if you did, would you want to use your personal savings?) or you could seek outside financing.

Instead of reaching into your personal savings, what if you decided to issue stock? Perhaps you have previously expressed this idea to friends and family members who are familiar with your business and product. They have witnessed how popular your lemonade is, and they believe in you and would be more than happy to invest in your company. Let's assume that if you were to issue stock, you would have around 250 people that would want to participate – a mixture of friends and family. But how can we arrive at a value for your stock, essentially, the value that each person will pay to own one share of your company?

The first step would be for you to arrive at an overall value for your business. You would add up the value of all of your assets (e.g., your vehicle, mixing machines, generators, lemonade stand, cash) and then subtract any debts that you owe on the business (e.g., bank loans). This figure will essentially give you a net value of your business. For example, if you were to sell your vehicle, mixing machines and the like, we estimate you would have about $15,000. However, you have a $5,000 loan remaining on your vehicle that you would have to pay off. You are now left with $10,000 as the liquidating value of your company. We then take this figure ($10,000) and divide it by the number of people who want to invest in the stock of your company, which is 250. Doing the math, each share of your company would be worth $40.

Each of your investors (those 250 people) gives you $40 in exchange for a piece of your business. In total, you receive an influx of $10,000, which you subsequently use to make the necessary upgrades to your lemonade business. In return, you provide each investor with a stock certificate.

That certificate explains that they now own 1 share out of 250 shares of your company, each share worth whatever the company is valued at, which is currently $40 per share. This stock certificate allows your investors, at any time, to sell their share back to you for the market value. Now, even though they gave you $40 and they received a stock certificate, the value of that certificate is based, in part, on the value of your company that we already determined ($10,000).

The thing is, the value of your business could change day to day. For example, let's assume that 6 months later, even after making the necessary upgrades, your business is not doing as well as you had hoped. Perhaps an extended storm system has prevented the downtown lunch crowd from going outside and, on top of this, certain sports teams have gone on strike, meaning you no longer have sporting venues to sell your product at. As a result, your lemonade sales have plummeted.

The storm system and sports strike mean your sales have plummeted and as a result, your business has not been generating cash. Perhaps because of this lack of cash, you have not been able to service your generators and so they are starting to deteriorate. Also, one of your coolers has broken and your vehicle has depreciated in value.

For the sake of argument, let's assume that after running through the calculations, it is determined that your liquidating value is now $8,000. In order to determine what each share of stock is now worth, we divide $8,000 by the 250 outstanding shares to arrive at a per share value of $32. If one of your original investors came to you at this point asking to sell back their stock certificate, you would give them $32. This means they actually would have lost $8 by investing in your company, as they initially invested $40. That may not seem like too large of a loss, but imagine if an investor owned hundreds or thousands of shares in your company. The losses could be quite high.

However, after another 6 months, your family and friends have stuck by you and no one has cashed in their certificates. They believed in you and had faith that you would succeed. Over the past 6 months, the weather has cleared up and the sports teams settled their strike. In fact, there are even more people out for lunch enjoying the beautiful weather and even more people attending games after the long break. These people are loving the upgrades you made to your business and you have sold a lot of lemonade, more than you could have imagined.

As a result, your company has experienced an influx of cash from these sales. You were able to fix up your generators and your vehicle so well that they've even increased in value.

You decide to calculate your liquidating value by determining the amount of cash you would receive for your assets and then subtracting debts. You figure out that your company is now worth $15,000, so when you divide this by the 250 outstanding shares, you see that your shares are now worth $60 each. If a current stock owner came to you to sell their stock, they would receive $60, a $20 increase from their original investment. In the preceding example our investor owned only one share and made $20 from that share. However, if, in this hypothetical example, an investor owned hundreds or thousands of shares of your company stock, the gains could be substantial. For example, if an investor owned 1,000 shares they would have made investment earnings of $20,000.

Let us briefly touch on a real-world example of how stock price valuation can be rather difficult.

"Tech" Bubble of the 1990s

Stock price valuation can be said to have developed through the analysis of "brick and mortar" type companies. That is, companies with physical assets such as buildings (the brick), machinery (the mortar), and other items that have actual value associated with them and can be sold off at a later date. Of course, in our lemonade stand example there is no physical building, but there are assets like your vehicle, mixing machines, and trailer, that have value associated with them and could be liquidated or sold. On the other hand, there are companies that might not have a lot of physical assets (the brick) by the very nature of their business. Case in point, technology or internet companies.

A big reason why our country experienced a substantial stock market downturn in the late 1990s and early 2000s was due to a so-called "tech bubble." With the advent of the Internet, new technology companies started sprouting up all over the place. Often, these internet companies would have a small office location (perhaps being leased and not even owned by the company), a few computers and office staff like computer programmers.

A good majority of their business, if not all of it, was done virtually, through the Internet. We did not have lemonade mixing machines, vehicles, and the like to value and then arrive at a stock price (i.e., the brick and mortar). So, how were the stock prices of these companies valued?

This is where a large part of the problem arose. At the time, internet companies were sprouting up left and right. Each new dot-com seemed to be the next new great idea. How attractive these companies made themselves appear (mainly through advertising campaigns) would contribute largely to the stock price associated with that company. In fact, these companies wouldn't necessarily even have any product or record of sales, yet investors were so excited for the idea that they were willing to pay very high stock prices to invest in these companies. Unfortunately for many of these investors, the day of reckoning came.

These were such exciting times with the introduction of this new technology called "*the Internet*" or "*Online.*" For a three-year period starting in 1997 investors were buying up anything even vaguely associated with the Internet. However, within a few short years it was hard not to find a publicly traded Internet company whose stock value was not down at least 75% and that had not undergone major restructuring such as laying off workers and trimming expenses. Investors were wild about the promise of these new internet stocks, yet the financial markets had not yet found a proper way of valuing these new technology companies.

Although the above example of a lemonade stand and our subsequent discussion surrounding the dot-com bubble are provided as purely illustrative, they give you an idea of the thinking and tedious analysis that goes into how stock prices are determined. Of course, in reality, stock price valuation is a much more complex, elaborate undertaking that usually requires complicated financial statements and complex formulas and algorithms. These discussions are outside the scope of this book. For now, we'll keep it as simple as possible.

One of the main purposes of this book is to provide you with the absolute essentials of investing, and armed with this basic understanding, you will be able to branch off and focus on more specific topics. For those of you who want to research stock pricing and valuation a bit further, I suggest you explore the following topics: *Capital Asset Pricing Model* (CAPM), *Dividend Discount Model* and *Internal Rate of Return*. These are somewhat advanced subjects related to stock valuation but will allow you to further your knowledge with respect to stock pricing.

Now that you understand the basics of stock pricing, I would like to introduce to you what I consider to be one of the most important tenants of a basic stock education: separating value and growth.

Value and Growth – Toilet Paper and Electronics

There are potentially thousands upon thousands of stocks traded daily in the United States through physical stock exchanges as well as electronic ones. It would not seem probable that an individual investor such as yourself would be able to analyze each of these

CONSUMER STAPLES: GOODS THAT PEOPLE ARE UNWILLING TO CUT OUT OF THEIR BUDGETS, REGARDLESS OF THEIR FINANCIAL CONDITION.

thousands of companies, value the companies, determine a stock price, then calculate whether the company's stock price is currently undervalued or overvalued, and decide to invest your money, or not. In fact, the number of stocks available for investment are so diverse that even professional investors can feel overwhelmed. Fret not, there are tools at our disposal that attempt to clear up the process. One concept is to take all of thousands of stocks and divide them into two categories: *Value (toilet paper)* and *Growth (electronics)*. Let's expand on this idea.

There are some goods and services that a good majority of people will continuously purchase, regardless of our economic situation. These can include things like food, medicine, and household items (e.g., toilet

CONSUMER DISCRETIONARY: GOODS AND SERVICES CONSIDERED NON-ESSENTIAL, BUT DESIRABLE IF INCOME IS SUFFICIENT TO PURCHASE THEM.

paper). These types of products are necessities for our lives and are commonly referred to as *consumer staples*. Again, these are products we need for daily living and we will lump these stocks into the *Value* category.

On the other hand, there are items that can be considered *non-necessities*. These are things that people buy because they *want* them, rather than based on an essential need. They may make us happy, but our daily lives are not dependent on them. These would include items such as meals at a restaurant, high-end clothing, and luxury goods (e.g., electronics). Since these items are not required for our day-to-day living needs, we can refer to them as *consumer discretionary* products and we will place these types of companies in the *Growth* category.

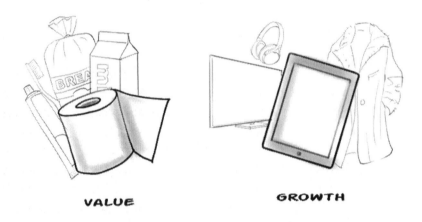

VALUE   GROWTH

Keeping these two concepts in mind, *Consumer Staples (Value)* and *Consumer Discretionary (Growth)*, let's briefly touch on an economic discussion, after which we will circle back to the *Value* and *Growth* concept.

Basic Economic Discussion

I imagine it would be no surprise for me to say that our economy ebbs and flows. The US economy has periods in which it is roaring along (what we will call an *expansion* phase) and periods in which the economy is barely chugging along (what we will call a *contraction* phase). Perhaps we can relate our economy to that of a car engine. If you cruise along at 100 mph for too long, your engine could overheat and break down, requiring you to pull over to the side of the road to give your engine time to cool down. On the contrary, if you are traveling too slowly, you may not get to your destination as quickly as you want to and you are not getting the most of your car's output. Finding this balance is essentially the root of economic policy and can often be more of an art than a science – there is usually no perfect and clear answer.

Economic Expansion

Our economy works cyclically. When we're in an expansion phase, the economy grows to a point where it becomes unsustainable, and then it begins to contract. Let me show you why. In an expansion, interest rates are usually low and this means loans are more affordable. In essence, it becomes less expensive to finance various capital projects whether that be the purchasing of a home or taking out a loan to start a new business. As a result, we may see an increase in new business start-ups (i.e., new business loans being issued). These new businesses will more than likely require employees and so we can expect to see hiring start to pick up, which generally leads to a lower unemployment rate. As more people are entering the workforce, people tend to have more money. When we have more money, we start to purchase more goods and services. With more people buying goods and services, it can be expected that the costs of those goods and services will increase. This is a basic tenant of economics and tends to hold true in the real world – that is, as demand for a product increases, so too will the price of that product.

Let me briefly explain how this works before I move on to explain where contraction comes in. Imagine that you have put an item up for sale on Craigslist and you are inundated with people calling you to buy your product. Left and right, you have people making you offers. Are you going to be forced to lower your price when so many people want (i.e., demand) it? Most likely not and, in fact, you will probably be able to increase your asking price. This increase in the costs of goods and services can be referred to as *inflation*, and it is typical to see inflation during an expansion phase.

It is these sorts of economic indicators (e.g., inflation, unemployment, business start-ups) that we can watch to get an idea as to where our economy was, is and could be going. Eventually though, the party ends.

Economic Contraction

Just like a car traveling at 100 mph for too long, our economy will not be able to sustain this expansionary growth phase and it will "burn out." In an attempt to cool off the economy and prevent a "burn out," we start to see an increase in overall interest rates. This increase in interest rates usually starts with actions taken by the Federal Reserve

INFLATION: A SUSTAINED INCREASE IN THE GENERAL LEVEL OF PRICES FOR GOODS AND SERVICES.

Board who dictates interest rate policy in the US. Essentially, if they (the FRB) raise interest rates that the government charges, then most interest rates in the economy follow suit (e.g., interest earned on cash accounts, loans), and this is what starts the overall general increase in interest rates throughout our economy.

Increasing interest rates usually slow down an economy – in essence, having the effect of pulling our foot off of the gas to slow down the car. This is because when interest rates begin to rise, loans generally become more expensive. As a result, people are less likely to want to take out loans to finance new car purchases, housing purchases and new businesses. As a result, we see fewer loans being issued. This in turn means fewer new businesses will start up, which could then lead to a tightening job market (i.e., not as many new jobs being offered).

Also, when interest rates increase, other loans become more expensive as well. People stop buying big ticket items like cars and homes because their loans will be too expensive. This can have negative ramifications that reach out all throughout our economy. For example, when home purchases decrease, it means we have fewer people living in homes and fewer people visiting the local hardware store to purchase housing goods. As a result, hardware companies may experience a decrease in sales. With a decrease in sales, these businesses may start to take action to keep their operations running smoothly. Perhaps these businesses will stop future expansions, forego pay raises or even end up firing employees.

The expansion, contraction and subsequent repeating of the process is the general nature of the ebb and flow of our economy. Of course, some periods may last longer than others. For example, the 1990's saw an incredible economic expansion followed by a tech bubble and then there was the 2008 financial crisis, which brought in a prolonged period of economic contraction.

But what does that have to do with stocks? And what about Value and Growth?

Well, during times of an economic expansion when unemployment is low and more and more people are making money, we are usually able to afford, or at least have the money to spend on, *discretionary* items such as high-end clothing or electronics (i.e., growth stocks). As we just learned, the prices charged for these items will likely be high, and the companies making those products will most likely see their sales increase (perhaps dramatically). This increase in sales can be reflected in an increasing stock price. *(Think back to our lemonade stand example and what happened when our lemonade business started to see positive results. The stock price per share started to increase.)*

And what about *consumer staple* items during this expansionary phase of the economy? What happens to the products we purchase as part of our daily living? Will we start to forego the purchasing of household items such as toilet paper? I certainly hope not! These companies will more than likely experience positive results as well; however, the products produced by these companies usually do not have high production costs and, as a result, may not have as high of a selling price. So, even though value-related companies might also experience an increase in sales, the price per share of the companies may not be as "lucrative" as growth related companies. But, what happens to these same companies (i.e., value and growth) when our economy enters a contraction phase?

One notable indicator of an economic contraction is the unemployment rate. Perhaps we see a substantial increase in the unemployment rate due to layoffs as well as the lack of new business startups (i.e., fewer jobs). When the unemployment rate is increasing, consumers are not making as much money, if any. As a result, consumers may start to tighten their budgets and forego purchasing *non-necessity* items like *Consumer Discretionary* products (i.e., growth stocks). Products such as high-end clothing and electronics, although nice to have, would not be a main concern at this point. However, most households, jobless or not, will continue to purchase products such as household items and medicine—what we call *consumer staples* (i.e., value stocks).

Value and Growth Stocks

From our brief economic discussion we can start to uncover some new ideas related to stock investing. That is to say, no matter what economic condition we may be in (*expansion* or *contraction*) products that are a necessity for our day-to-day living will continue to be purchased, perhaps not as often or not in bulk, but people will still continue to purchase them. These are value products, so when you think of value I want you to imagine a roll of toilet paper.

VALUE

Now the thing is, toilet paper tends to have low costs associated with its production and as a result, it is usually a rather inexpensive purchase. Given this, the potential profit for a company when selling toilet paper is probably low (at least when compared to more lucrative products such as electronics). An investment in a value-oriented company might not produce the higher potential returns you're used to hearing about from growth companies. We've seen that people will still continue to buy toilet paper whether we are in expansion or contraction, so the price of value-oriented companies' stocks are less influenced by economic cycles.

Growth stocks, on the other hand, can have dramatically different features. When you think of growth product, imagine a tablet. The production of a tablet may have high costs associated with it (e.g., research and development, technical expertise, many parts) so they will usually have high retail price tags when compared to toilet paper products. As a result, we can expect that the profit potential for an electronics manufacturer will be much higher than a toilet paper company. But because growth product prices are heavily influenced by economic cycles, the companies that primarily produce these products (growth-oriented companies) experience much greater expansion and contraction with the economy.

GROWTH

That's great, but what does it have to do with stock investing? Well, growth and value stocks behave in such different ways that the type of stocks we invest in actually change the investment strategy. Let me explain…

Investing in Stocks

At the beginning of this chapter I explained what stocks are and how their prices are generally determined, but what I didn't tell you is how stock investing actually generates money. As stated earlier, when you buy a stock you are *giving* your money to a particular company who then provides you an IOU (e.g., a stock certificate). Generally speaking, you can hold onto that stock certificate as long as you like and in fact there are stories of families passing on their stock certificates to future generations.

The value of the stock certificate can change moment by moment, day by day based on the underlying value of the company (think back to our lemonade stand example). This means that you could pay $50 for the certificate and the very next day it could be worth $75 or even lose all of its value. Then again, a few days, months, or even years later that same stock certificate you are holding onto could be worth more or less. You won't actually gain or lose money until you actually sell your stock back to the company (more on this in our tax discussion). So, what does all of this have to do with value and growth stocks?

Simply put, when the economy is performing positively, consumers (you and I) will continue to purchase toilet paper and may even decide to spend some of our hard-earned money on a tablet. However, when the economy starts to deteriorate, we may hold off on purchasing luxury items such as a tablet, yet we continue to purchase toilet paper – or at least I hope so!

This means that during an economic expansion an investment in a growth stock might have the potential to produce greater returns when compared to a value company. However, in an economic contraction, the growth companies might see a more dramatic decrease in their stock price whereas value oriented investments might not see such a dramatic decrease. The following charts should present these ideas in a visual manner.

The first chart shows the hypothetical performance of what might be expected for the performance of growth and value stocks over the long-term.

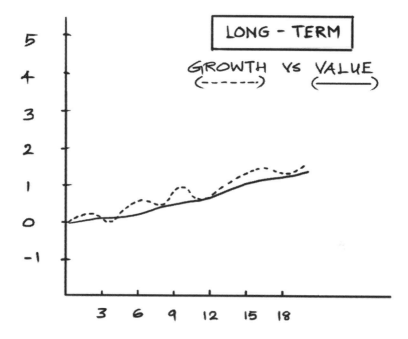

Over the long-term, growth stocks have tended to outperform (made a larger return for investors) when compared to value stocks. Once again, this should make sense given that growth companies have substantial profits based on the luxury items they produce. At the same time, value companies produce products that, although they aren't as profitable, are less impacted by economic conditions. But let's look at what happens to the performance of the two categories when we narrow our time frame.

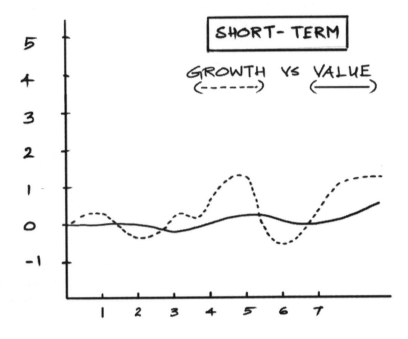

It should be noted that in the short-term, growth stocks (in the above chart) have a few wild fluctuations in value both up and down. This means that, in the short-term, had you invested in the above growth stocks, you could have seen your investment money increase and decrease in value quite dramatically. Value stocks, on the other hand, were more stable. That's not to say that value stocks didn't fluctuate, but the fluctuations weren't as great as growth stock fluctuations (both up and down).

One thing that should be clear with the above charts is that over the long run, growth stocks have the potential to earn an investor more money, but there could also be wild fluctuations in the value of growth stocks during the short-term. On the contrary, value stocks may see less volatility (when compared to growth stocks), but also may not provide as much potential return in the long term. There is no guarantee that all growth stocks and all value stocks will act in the same manner as laid out above, but historically the above concepts seem to play out.

Now, another potential benefit of investing in stocks, apart from the growth in value of the stock certificate (i.e., the *IOU*), is that of dividends.

Dividends

A company you have invested in might have had an incredible few weeks of sales and, after covering all its business expenses, might have money left over. The company, as we touched on in our lemonade stand example, might use that *excess* money to reinvest into improving operations, creating a better product (such as through research & development) or simply save the money. Another option for the company is to share its success with its stockholders by issuing them dividends.

Dividends can be a cash payment, additional shares of stock or other property. The easiest way to think of dividends is as interest earned on your stock certificate—a *bonus* if you will. You still own the stock and can benefit from any increase in value, but you might also experience the added benefit of a dividend payment.

For example, let's assume you invested $10,000 into the stock *ABC Company,* who pays a 2% annual dividend every quarter. This means every three months (i.e., every quarter) you should expect to receive an additional $50 in cash. What you decide to do with the dividend is up to you. Perhaps you request the cash be sent to you by check or maybe you request the money simply be used to purchase more shares of the company (what is commonly referred to as *reinvesting dividends*).

Not all companies issue dividends, and those that do are often mature companies. If you think about it, this should make sense. For example, new companies usually need to use the monies from operations to expand their production, hire new personnel, expand their marketing presence and a host of other business costs. Mature companies, which have been around for years, decades or even centuries, often have reached a large enough size that they can simply focus on specifics of the business, such as research & development in hopes of creating a new and exciting product (think of Apple®). Often, retirees who have invested in stock will usually invest in the stock of well-established, mature companies who consistently pay cash dividends. These cash dividends can then be paid out directly to the retirees (usually deposited directly into their bank accounts), who use those cash dividends as a form of supplemental income.

Without getting lost in the weeds, please think of dividends as a form of interest in regard to stock investing and remember they can be very beneficial.

Sizes of Companies – Small, Medium, & Large

Companies are usually classified as either being small, medium, or large in size. Often, the size classification relates to the asset value of the company. Think back to our lemonade stand example. In that example, it was clearly a small business consisting of a car, one lemonade stand and you, the owner. But what about lemonade stand businesses that have thousands of stands throughout the country with employees at each one? That would clearly be a much larger company.

It may stand to reason that the larger a company is, the more resources it has at its disposal. Consider a large manufacturing company that has numerous manufacturing plants located throughout the United States. These manufacturing plants might be filled with all sorts of machinery, some very complex. Additionally, some of these large companies may employ thousands of individuals in numerous positions. We will most likely see departments like Human Resources, Legal, and Customer Service as well as plant operations personnel. There will likely also be many levels of management. The point is, large companies usually have lots of resources. If an economic contraction is starting to take shape and times are getting rough for businesses, large companies have more options with which to weather the storm when compared to their smaller counterparts.

A larger company could liquidate some of their machinery to acquire cash, close down plants to save on costs, or lay off personnel without disrupting operations. Larger companies tend to have grown up over time, which means their products are popular and can often withstand economic instability. As a result, obtaining additional capital from other means (e.g., bank loans, issuing bonds, issuing stocks) might be easier because of their successful track record and assets. In general, this means that larger companies can typically withstand fluctuations in the economy much better than smaller businesses. Stocks in larger companies may not have the potential for *rapid* growth over time, but they are generally more stable and less risky.

Some companies are small by their very nature and may remain successful that way, but some may be small because they are still in the early stages of their business life. Small companies are generally new to their respective markets, and if they produce a product that consumers want, their profit potential is great and their stock price might subsequently increase. Essentially, smaller companies have greater potential for investment returns.

However, small companies may present a host of risks based on economic conditions. For example, small companies may not have as many resources to help them stay afloat in the event of an economic downturn. They usually don't have as much machinery they can liquidate to generate cash. They usually have only essential personnel to meet day-to-day operations, so termination of employees would drastically affect their operations and so is not a viable cash-saving strategy. Unlike their larger counterparts, these small companies have to fight to get their product into the market and have not "proven" themselves yet, so they are less likely to be able to raise funds (through loans, issuing stocks, or issuing bonds) when they are low on cash. This means that although stocks in smaller businesses typically have higher potential returns, they are riskier than larger businesses.

Although the characteristics we have listed are not all-encompassing and may not apply to every company, what I am trying to get across to you is the fact that, in general, smaller companies pose greater risk when compared to large companies. Are there some small companies that, in the end, outperform their larger counterparts? Sure. Are there some large companies that regardless of how well they run their business might have some sort of accounting scandal come to light that ends in the company's demise? Yes, this can and has happened. However, in general, over time, smaller companies are riskier, while larger companies are more stable.

Stock Grid

Let's take this opportunity to introduce a hopefully easy-to-understand illustration that summarizes a good portion of the information, pertaining to stocks, which we have been discussing:

STOCKS

VALUE	BLEND	GROWTH	
			LARGE
			MEDIUM
			SMALL

The above stock grid allows us to get an immediate idea of the characteristics of the stock that is being discussed. You'll usually see stocks placed in one of these cells, so you can quickly see which categories the stock fits into. For example, let's assume that we are looking at two hypothetical stock tickers (XYZ and ABC).

STOCKS

VALUE	BLEND	GROWTH	
XYZ		ABC	LARGE
			MEDIUM
			SMALL

XYZ is listed in the most upper-left box, which represents a Large Value company. Stock ABC is listed in the most upper-right hand box, which represents a Large Growth company.

After our prior discussion of value versus growth, you should now be able to almost immediately realize a few key characteristics. For example, XYZ makes toilet paper and ABC makes electronics.[13] This could suggest that stock ABC represents more risk, but also potentially greater return given that it is a growth-type company. Over the long term, ABC stock may produce positive gains over and above that of XYZ, but in the short-term, ABC may see wild fluctuations.

As a growth company, the success of ABC may be heavily reliant on how well the overall economy is performing. After all, in an economic contraction, if people have less money they may forego purchasing "luxury" goods that tend to be produced by growth companies. However, if the economy is roaring, people may have more money, and if company ABC has a product that a lot of us want and like (in high demand), perhaps the stock has a chance of providing a substantial return.

On the other hand, stock XYZ, which is a large value company, might not be able to produce as great of returns during an economic boom. However, during an economic contraction, the products produced by XYZ may continue to sell regardless of what the economic conditions are. As a result, the losses from an investment in XYZ might not be as substantial as ABC.

The different between XYZ and ABC is in the type of products the companies produce. But what if we look at two companies that produce the same types of goods?

---

13 Value stocks can incorporate businesses other than toilet paper manufacturers and growth stocks can represent companies that make non-electronic products and/or services. However, for our basic discussion I would like you to think of toilet paper when we discuss value and electronics when we discuss growth.

STOCKS

	VALUE	BLEND	GROWTH	
	ZZZ			LARGE
				MEDIUM
	WWW			SMALL

In the above illustration, we see two companies: ZZZ and WWW. What can we deduce from this simple chart?

One of the first concepts that should pop out to you is that both companies are classified as value companies. This means these two companies are most likely in the business of producing consumer staple products.

Another piece of information that should stand out is that even though they are both classified as value stocks, WWW is considered a small company whereas ZZZ is considered a large company. So, even though they are both within the value category, one of them presents more risk (and the potential for greater reward). As we learned previously, there are a host of reasons why a smaller company typically presents more risk than its larger counterparts. As such, in the end, WWW would likely be the riskier investment.

Indices

I image that most of us hear on the nightly news about how the stock markets performed for the day. These blurbs probably sound similar to, "The Dow Jones was up 45 points to 9,856, the NASDAQ was down 3 points to 3,456, and the S&P closed flat at 1,500." So, what does all of this mean besides some sort of vague indication of the stock market either going up, down, or remaining flat?

You know that there are potentially thousands upon thousands of stocks available for investment. A starting point for making sense of these investments is to divide them into two camps: value stocks and growth stocks, or put another way, toilet paper and electronics. But since there are so many, we need a way to track how these categories are performing overall. That's where the Dow Jones, NASDAQ, and S&P come in. They are indices that track the overall performance of stocks in their category.

These indices track the various categories of stock (i.e., value and growth) usually on a daily basis – moment by moment. They essentially provide us real-time information as to how value and growth stocks are performing, and we can look at the historical records of these indices to see what has happened in the past to perhaps provide us indications of where we are headed into the future. For example, if we see that growth companies have been performing well for quite some time, then that might suggest to us that the economy has been in an economic expansion and perhaps may eventually start to cool off. If this is the case, which companies might experience the more dramatic decrease in value? Growth stocks. This means that you may want to avoid growth stocks and instead focus on value stocks or an entirely different asset class (i.e., cash or bonds).

So what exactly do the Dow Jones, NASDQ, and S&P do? Probably one of the most widely known and tracked indices is the Dow Jones Industrial Average (DJIA).

The companies listed and tracked by the DJIA are the 30 largest stocks traded on the New York Stock Exchange and represent the value category (i.e., Large Toilet Paper companies).

The NASDAQ tracks the performance of large, growth oriented stocks – large electronic companies. Finally, the S&P 500 can be considered a blended index that tracks the performance of some of our nation's largest value- and growth-oriented companies.

The **NASDAQ** is a stock market index of the common stocks (and similar securities) listed on the NASDAQ stock market. Along with the DJIA and S&P 500, it is one of the most followed indices in the US. I want you to think of the NASDAQ as representing growth companies (i.e., tablet companies).

The **DJIA** is one of the oldest and most watched indices in the world and tracks 30 significant stocks traded on the New York Stock Exchange (NYSE) and NASDAQ. I want you to think of the DJIA as representing value companies (i.e., toilet paper stocks).

The **S&P 500** is an index of 500 stocks seen as a leading indicator of U.S. equities. I want you to view the S&P 500 as a blended index. That is, the S&P 500 will represent both value and growth companies (both toilet paper and electronics).

Now you will know what is being presented to you on your next evening drive home from work. The DJIA represents large toilet paper companies, the NASDAQ represents large electronic companies, and the S&P 500 represents the performance of large toilet paper and electronic companies. It really is this simple!

On this note, following the indices on a daily basis might be appropriate for active investors who are constantly keeping an eye on the stock market and perhaps trading stocks on a daily basis. For the rest of us, checking in every now and then (whether that be daily, weekly, monthly or a few times a year) should suffice in allowing us to have a broader understanding of where our economy, the stock market, and even our own investments are.

Last, and on a hopefully somewhat entertaining note, is what we commonly hear referred to as *Bear Markets* and *Bull Markets*. As you become more involved in the investing world (e.g., stock market), you will often here references to a *Bull Market* and *Bear Market*. These are terms used to describe how the stock markets have been and are performing. A *Bull Market,* means the stock market is generally performing well and is increasing in value (i.e., stocks are growing in value). *Bear Markets* refer to investment markets that are experiencing a decline in value (i.e., stocks overall are decreasing in value). The reason behind these terms relates to the way in which the corresponding animals attack. When a bull attacks it raises its head to launch its horns *upwards*, hence a *rising* stock market. Bears generally attack by swiping their paws in a *downward* motion, hence a *declining* market.

Summary

As we near the end of our stock discussion, I truly hope that the preceding chapter has provided you a newer understanding of stock investing. We have digested quite a bit of information surrounding stocks and for many of you, this is your first real introduction into stock investing.

Sure, the world of stocks may seem perplexing, but recalling some basic principles should help you to make sense of it all.

We started off our discussion of stocks with a brief explanation of how stocks are essentially an IOU. That when investing in stocks you are in essence handing over your money to a corporation, who in turn provides you a stock certificate (the IOU). Your hope is that the corporation uses your money to improve their business, which in turn increases the value of your stock certificate.

We then discussed how stock prices can vary greatly, with some stocks being offered at only pennies per share while other stocks may be worth hundreds of thousands of dollars per share. Why is this? Of course, the actual process of calculating a stock price is quite complicated, but it is typically based on the total value of the company's assets, divided over the number of stocks they've issued.

When it comes to the world of stock investing, I want you to think of stocks as being separated into two categories: value and growth, or toilet paper and electronics. Even though this may seem rather elementary, it is also a fundamental concept of stock investing and it does work!

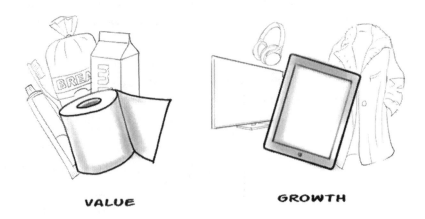

VALUE   GROWTH

Additionally, we spent some time discussing how each category acts during different economic scenarios. That is to say that no matter what the economy is doing, we will continue to buy toilet paper type products (i.e., *consumer staples*). However, when it comes to electronic type products (i.e., *consumer discretionary*), we may delay those purchases during tough economic times and wait until the economy improves.

These basic characteristics of value and growth stocks indicate to us that growth stocks may provide us greater potential to make money, but may also lose money in rough economic times. In contrast, value stocks might provide less volatility, but also lower potential for returns.

Another important aspect of stock investments is to categorize companies based on their size. Although not guaranteed, it stands to reason that the larger a company is, the better positioned it might be to weather an economic contraction. So, if we have two companies in the same category (e.g., a small toilet paper company and a large toilet paper company), it would stand to reason that the smaller toilet paper company would pose more risk to an investor, yet has the potential for greater gain as well.

Finally, we discussed three of the most common stock indices. These three indices (DJIA, NASDAQ, and S&P 500) are usually quoted on nightly television news and radio programming. They provide us a glimpse into how value and growth stocks performed over the course of a day, week, month, year, and even decades. It may not be necessary, and in fact might be a detriment for most of us, to track these indices on a daily basis, but if we are at least aware of these indices, what they represent and how they have performed historically, we may be able to arrive at a better investment decision or at least understand our current investments a bit better.

At the beginning of this chapter we presented an empty stock bucket. After the last few pages of our stock discussion, we can now fill up our bucket and celebrate your understanding of investing and in this instance, stocks.

Chapter 5

Buckets Recap

Up to this point, we've focused on what I consider to be the foundational building blocks of a solid financial education: cash, bonds, and stocks. Not only that, but for many of you this has been your first real exposure to investing concepts, and so it would suit us well to briefly recap what we have been discussing.

If you are anything like me, investments were, at one point, a complex topic. When we started off our conversation in Chapter 1, I asked that you make a list of the types of investments you believe are available to you. It probably included at least one of the following:

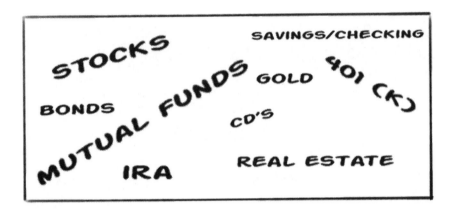

Until now, the world of investing may have seemed this complex—an endless list of knowns and unknowns, of confusing investing ideas, fancy words, and intricate subjects. But, as you now know, it doesn't have to be this way.

No matter what you think you might know about investing, no matter what you hear on local radio or television programing, simply remember that investments will fall into one of three buckets:

Remembering this concept we can then recall that each bucket has investments within it:

Again, you will most likely hear friends, acquaintances, television, and radio programming and perhaps even family members discussing other types of investments such as real estate or gold and usually with fervor. Forget about them. For our purposes, they are outlier investments that only complicate this introduction.

You may also hear about topics that are in fact related to investments, such as options or short selling. These are not investments in and of themselves, but rather ways of trading certain investments. These topics are outside the scope of this book and really won't serve you well when obtaining a basic understanding of investments. Again, I stress the importance for you to remember the three buckets and for now, keep it this simple!

Housecleaning – Asset Classes

At this point, we need to discuss a bit of housecleaning. Given that the ultimate goal of this book is to explain and educate investors on the basics of investing, I have referred to investment types as *buckets*. These are images that I hope you will find easy to recall in the future, long after you have put this book down. However, going forward we will refer more and more to the buckets as *assets* or *asset classes*.

Simply put, cash is an asset, bonds are an asset, and stocks are an asset. Asset classes, then, are groups or types of assets. So, "cash" is an asset class while a checking account is an asset within the "cash" asset class. This is a more appropriate description of what the three buckets represent and if you can start to incorporate this sort of financial literacy in your dialogue, you will build credibility. Plus, and perhaps more importantly, is that when listening to financial radio and television or reading financial articles, you will most likely hear talk of asset classes, which you now know refers to our buckets.

Having a solid understanding of the simple fact that we now have three asset classes of investing, we need to be able to further define those various asset classes as well as being able to explain what types of investments are within each class and the differences between the asset classes. Why would you invest in one asset class over another? Or should you invest a bit in all three asset classes?

Believe it or not, we have already answered these questions, and more, through the last few chapters. As you know, these asset classes have a risk-level hierarchy such that cash is the most conservative and stocks are the most aggressive (with bonds being in the middle).

Another important concept as it relates to the three asset classes is time horizon. If you know your own time horizon, you can often determine which investment class you should focus your attention towards.

Cash Asset Class

As discussed prior, the cash bucket is the most conservative of the three asset classes and can include investments such as checking accounts, savings accounts, certificates of deposit, and money market mutual funds. When compared to the other asset classes, cash provides the least amount of risk (i.e., possibility of loss of money) yet the lower potential return, or *growth.*

The primary goal of cash investments is to preserve the principal amount invested and allow easy access to the funds, or what you now know as *liquidity.* Put another way, cash investing is for those individuals who do not want to risk losing any of their money and instead opt for "safety" even though this absence of risk ensures very small interest payments.

Investors with short-term time frames (generally one year or less) will often consider investing in cash investments. This is because other asset classes could potentially lose a substantial amount of money within a year's timeframe and not recover by the time you need the money. Cash, on the other hand, is supposed to just sit there and grow very slowly over time through usually minuscule interest payments. The below illustration summarizes the cash investments we have discussed up to this point.

Bond Asset Class

For many of you, this was your first introduction to bond investing and I hope it was somewhat entertaining. Bond discussions can have a "draining" effect of sorts. Even still, bonds can play a critical part in an investment portfolio.

When compared to cash investments, bonds present a whole new set of risks. As we discussed prior, some of these risks include *default*, *opportunity*, and *interest rate* risk (i.e., the teeter-totter).

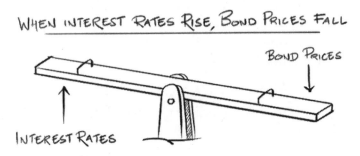

WHEN INTEREST RATES RISE, BOND PRICES FALL

BOND PRICES

INTEREST RATES

(The above illustration represents one of the most basic concepts of bond investing – as interest rates rise, the value of bonds decreases.)

It is because you as an investor are accepting these added risks (when investing in bonds) that you can expect your interest payments to be substantially larger. In fact, the interest paid out by bonds is often used as supplemental income for retirees.

There are quite a few characteristics that most bond investments share (e.g., *maturity*, *interest payment*), but there are actually many different types of bonds. The below illustrations should encapsulate for you the types of bond investments you will most likely encounter:

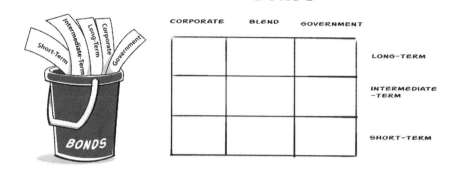

Stock Asset Class

Lastly, we come to what some consider the "crème de la crème" of investing – stocks. Oh the images of grandeur and wealth that go through the minds of many when they think of stocks. And yet, some of us may also feel great fear – that investing in stocks can mean the loss of a substantial amount, if not all, of our investment.

The above statements are largely true. That is, stock investing can potentially create great gains, but the flipside is that there can also be great losses. They generally present the most risk amongst the three asset classes, but I do not want you to feel intimidated or turned off by stock investing. Although, as a whole, stocks are the riskiest asset class, there can be great diversity within the stock bucket (just like with cash and bonds).

When it comes to stock investing, think of stocks as being represented by two categories – value and growth – or as I like to remember them, *toilet paper* and *electronics*.

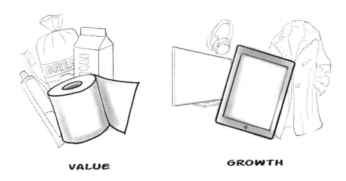

VALUE   GROWTH

Simply put, no matter what economic conditions are present (whether in an economic expansion or contraction), consumers will continue to purchase toilet paper. This means that value companies can usually expect continued sales regardless of economic conditions. However, the profit potential of toilet paper-related products, although perhaps consistent and less volatile over time, can be limited when compared to other more lucrative products such as electronics. This all means that, generally speaking, growth stocks (when compared to value stocks) have the potential to provide an investor with much larger growth, but also much larger losses.

As well, when it comes to stocks, we separate them into value and growth categories, but also further classify them based on the size of the company. That is, we classify stocks as being either small, medium, or large in size, as in the stock grid:

STOCKS

VALUE	BLEND	GROWTH	
			LARGE
			MEDIUM
			SMALL

Simply put, the smaller a company is, the more risk it generally poses. However, with this added risk comes the potential for greater reward (i.e., return).

While stocks can become rather complex when you look at all the thousands of possibilities and risk levels and types of investments, the main types of stock investments are summarized in this illustration:

Summary

The last five chapters of this book have been a presentation to you of what I consider to be the foundations of a basic knowledge of investing. We have covered the three main types of investment classes along with a discussion of the most common investments within each asset class. As I stated in Chapter 1, I ask that you forget the types of investments you think are out there in the investing world and instead focus on understanding the three asset classes we have discussed. I once again plead with you to keep it as simple as we have laid out.

Now, let us take our newfound knowledge and advance our discussion by introducing mutual funds and exchange-traded funds (ETFs).

Chapter 6

Mutual Funds & ETFs

In the previous chapters, we learned we can divide stocks into two categories: value and growth (or as you know them, "toilet paper" and "electronics"). Within those two categories, we can further classify stocks as small-, medium-, or large-cap. In other words, we can have large toilet paper companies or small toilet paper companies. This is a great start, but we are still left with potentially thousands of stocks within each of those categories. And we haven't even gotten to bonds.

We learned that bonds are issued by one of two entities: corporations or governments. Also, bonds are classified as short-, intermediate-, or long-term. This is a great way to simplify bond investing, but again that still leaves potentially hundreds, if not thousands, of bonds within each subsequent category for us to choose from. What are we to do?

One option is to engage in an analysis of each individual security within each of the subcategories. This would entail pouring through thousands of individual stocks within the value category or thousands of bonds within the corporate bond category. This would include an analysis of the various companies' assets and liabilities and then running calculations to determine a fair stock price—much like our lemonade stand example, but considerably more complicated. Do you really have the time, resources, and experience to do this?

Mutual funds do all of this for you and allow you to invest in the various asset classes. Let's start to talk about mutual funds.

Mutual Fund History

It is commonly accepted that the first "modern" mutual fund was introduced to U.S. investors sometime in the early 20th century. During this time, there were only a handful of mutual funds in existence, and they were generally accessible only to the wealthy. Fast forward to the 21st century, and there are some 10,000 mutual funds with roughly $15 trillion dollars of total assets.

With the rise of the mutual fund investment, you more than likely will be exposed to mutual funds at some point in your life. In fact, I am certain that a majority of you have already heard of or been exposed to mutual funds, most likely through a company sponsored 401(k) plan or Individual Retirement Account (IRA). But do you really understand how a mutual fund (or ETF) works? What exactly does it do, and how are these funds different from what we have been discussing? Let's try to explain the basics of mutual funds.

The Absolute Basics of a Mutual Fund

The basics of a mutual fund are this: you and potentially hundreds or even thousands of other investors deposit your money with a mutual fund company. The mutual fund company will usually have minimum investment amounts required for you to participate in the fund. These initial investment amounts can vary greatly. Some mutual funds may allow you to invest with no initial investment amount so long as you "promise" to establish an automatic investment plan, such as investing $50 per month. Yet other mutual funds may require initial investment amounts ranging anywhere from a few hundred dollars to tens of thousands of dollars.

Often, there will be hundreds or even thousands of investors, such as yourself, who will also make deposits with a mutual fund. The total of all of these deposits can be quite large with some mutual funds garnering hundreds of millions of dollars' worth of investor deposits. The management team at the mutual fund company will then use these monies to purchase various investments.

Given the usually sizeable amount of monies the mutual fund collects, it will be able to obtain broad *diversification* by investing in hundreds of different securities (i.e., stocks, bonds, and cash) on your behalf. You will own your proportional share of those investments.

The mutual fund company is usually comprised of a group of financial professionals whose job it is to use those pooled monies to invest in cash, bonds, and/or stocks on your behalf. For example, there may be a mutual fund called the *US Large Cap Value Stock Fund*. Using the knowledge we obtained in the prior chapters, the name itself tells us almost everything we need to know. This fund will invest in large value companies (i.e., large toilet paper companies). On the other hand, there may be a mutual fund called the *Long-Term Corporate Bond Fund*. Again, using the knowledge from our prior discussion, this fund would invest in long-term corporate bonds.[14]

Diversification

Let us assume that instead of investing in a mutual fund, you decided that you want to make your own investment choices. You decide to invest $10,000 in stocks. Furthermore, you decide you want to invest in the stock of large value companies. Your decision is to invest the $10,000 amongst three different companies (approximately $3,000 in each stock). What would happen to the value of your overall investment mix if just one of those companies were to experience dramatic failure (e.g., bankruptcy)? You could experience substantial losses. But what if you were able to diversify your $10,000 amongst dozens or hundreds of different value companies?

In this instance, if a handful of companies were to go bankrupt, you might not have such dramatic investment losses. However appealing this might sound, investing your $10,000 amongst dozens or hundreds of stocks is just not feasible. First, there are transaction costs associated with stock investing such as commissions (more on this in Chapter 12). Essentially, you pay a commission whenever you buy and then

---

14   The term capitalization simply refers to the size of a company's assets (e.g., is the company a small lemonade stand with few assets or a large lemonade stand with many assets?).

subsequently sell a stock. If you are purchasing dozens or hundreds of different stocks, these transaction costs could mount up rather quickly and in large sums. On the flipside, purchasing just a handful of stocks might not be the best approach either. After all, the value of your stock investments would be based on just a few companies. What happens if one or two go bankrupt? Mutual funds strike a balance between these two concepts providing broad diversification (i.e., diversification through many different stocks) and minimal transaction costs.

One of the main benefits of investing in a mutual fund is obtaining diversification from the start. Remember a mutual fund is essentially a big pot of pooled investor monies that usually equates to a rather sizeable sum (e.g., hundreds of millions of dollars or more). The management team of the mutual fund company will be able to use those large sums of monies to purchase hundreds of different securities.

For example, let's assume we have a mutual fund called *The Large-Cap Value Fund*. *The Large-Cap Value Fund*, as you now know, will invest in large value companies (i.e., large toilet paper companies). With such an abundance of investable resources (i.e., the pooled pot of investor monies), the management team will be able to invest in potentially hundreds of different large value companies. If you are proportionally invested in hundreds of companies, what would happen if a handful of those companies were to experience financial troubles and go bankrupt? You perhaps would experience very little investment losses. After all, those companies represented only a fractional proportion of your overall investment, which is dispersed amongst dozens (or even hundreds) of other companies.

The idea of diversification is one of the main benefits of investing in a mutual fund. Whereas an investor may not be able to obtain broad diversification on his/her own (particularly those of us without a lot of money to invest), by pooling his/her money with other investors—in the form of a mutual fund—broad diversification can be obtained.

CASH MUTUAL FUNDS

In Chapter 2, we discussed the particulars of money market mutual funds so let's try to keep our discussion of them brief. Money market mutual funds are generally the most common form of a mutual fund that is classified as a cash investment. The idea behind a money market mutual fund is to not lose money and instead to keep a net asset value (NAV) of $1.00 at all times. The investments inside the money market mutual fund can include certificates of deposit (CDs) and US Treasury Bills (T-Bills), as well as other cash investments, such as commercial paper. One of the main benefits of a money market mutual fund is the interest payment, which is typically paid on a monthly basis.

Keep in mind though, that since a money market mutual fund is characteristically less risky than bonds and stocks, it will have much lower interest payments, comparatively. However, as we now know, there are various investments within the cash bucket. In this regard, money markets may be considered risker and, as such, usually yield a higher rate of interest than the other cash investments (e.g., checking accounts, savings accounts, etc.).

BOND MUTUAL FUNDS

In Chapter 3, we spent some time discussing bond investments' characteristics, categories, risks, and potential rewards. Without delving back into that discussion, let's briefly recap a few key points. What you should now be able to recall is that bond investments typically are classified as either corporate or government and have maturities that are either short-, intermediate-, or long-term.

Corporate bonds generally present more risk than government bonds, and the longer the maturity of a bond (i.e., the longer your money is "locked up"), the more risk you will be exposed to.

I would bet my bottom dollar that, for most of the mutual funds you come across (in this instance, bond mutual funds), you will be able to determine what type of bonds they invest in simply by their names. For example, a bond mutual fund may be named the *Intermediate-Term Government Bond Fund*. This would imply the mutual fund invests in government bonds with maturities classified as intermediate-term. Another bond mutual fund may be called the *Short-Term Corporate Bond Fund*, which would entail a mutual fund that invests in bonds with short-term maturities issued by corporations. I presented you with a bond matrix that succinctly summarizes these points in a visual illustration.

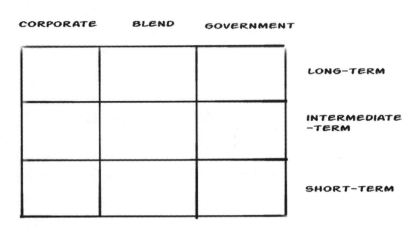

You will often find the above bond grid on most major financial websites (e.g., Morningstar, Yahoo! Finance) as well as financial reports. The bond grid will usually be blackened out (indicating the category of the bond fund). For example, a bond fund named *The Intermediate-Term Blended Bond Fund* would see the middle box in the bond grid blackened out. There may some derivation from the bond grid box (meaning, it won't look exactly the same), but more than likely, it will look very similar to the bond grid box presented above.

I mentioned blended mutual funds in prior chapters but did not delve too deeply into the topic. Now, I want to educate you on the concept of a blended mutual fund, in particular, a blended bond mutual fund.

In reality, bonds are either corporate or government; there is no middle ground. The concept of a blended bond is usually reserved for mutual funds. A bond mutual fund manager may decide to invest in both corporate and government bonds instead of strictly corporate bonds or strictly government bonds. In these instances, the bond mutual fund would be categorized as a blended mutual fund (i.e., it mixes both corporate and government bond investments). One of the ideas behind this type of investment is that a blended bond mutual fund may not be as risky as investing solely in corporate bonds, but also not as conservative as investing solely in government bonds.

STOCK MUTUAL FUNDS

In Chapter 4, we discussed stocks. Let's rehash a few key points. First, stocks can be classified as either value or growth. In this book, we symbolized value stocks as representing toilet paper and growth stocks representing electronics. Secondly, stocks can be classified by their size: small, medium, or large. We also mentioned blended stocks, which just like bonds, usually only exist in stock mutual funds. That is to say, stocks are usually either growth or value; there is no middle ground. Companies, over time and based on events, may fluctuate between the two, going from growth to value, but are usually one or the other.

A stock mutual fund manager may decide that investing solely in value or solely in growth is not appropriate, and as such, he/she may incorporate a mixture (i.e., blend) of the two stock styles. Whatever the case, the below stock grid is extremely helpful in making sense of the stock world and, in particular, stock mutual funds

STOCKS

VALUE	BLEND	GROWTH	
			LARGE
			MEDIUM
			SMALL

Just like bond mutual funds, you will usually be able to determine what type of stocks a particular mutual fund invests in based on its name. For example, a stock mutual fund may have a name like the *Small Cap Growth Fund*. We should now know this means you will be investing, through the fund manager, in stocks of small companies that are growth-oriented, or small electronic companies in our example. Another fund may be called the *Large Cap Blended Fund*, which would entail investments in both large value (i.e., large toilet paper companies) and large growth (i.e., large electronic companies).

ASSET ALLOCATION MUTUAL FUNDS

In Chapter 7 we will discuss the concept of asset allocation. However, we can touch on the basics of asset allocation and asset allocation mutual funds now.

Generally speaking, the younger we are and/or the more time we have before needing to access our invested money, the more we can choose riskier assets, such as stocks. However, as we get closer to when we actually plan to use the money, we might want to consider shifting our assets out of riskier investments (e.g., stocks) and moving those assets into more conservative investments (e.g., cash and/or bonds).

The mutual funds we have mentioned thus far usually invest in nothing more than their respective asset class. For example, a bond mutual fund will invest in bonds and a stock mutual fund will invest in stocks. There may be some variation in the types of bond or stock funds, such as a government bond fund investing in government bonds compared to a corporate bond fund investing in bonds issued by corporations. However, a bond fund will invest in bonds.

Asset allocation mutual funds, however, will invest a portion of your money into cash, bonds, and stocks. In essence, your money will be exposed to each bucket. Some of these asset allocations will be fixed. For example, there may be an asset allocation mutual fund that will invest 10% of your money into cash, 20% into bonds, and the remaining 70% into stocks. There might also be asset allocation funds that will adjust this mixture over time on your behalf. For example, there may be an asset allocation mutual fund called *The 2045 Asset Allocation Fund*.

Usually, with funds that have a target date in their names, the asset allocation will begin aggressive (i.e., more stock exposure) and then, as we approach the set date (in the above example, 2045), the mutual fund will invest more of the fund's monies into the more conservative asset classes (i.e., cash and bonds).

Asset allocation mutual funds are becoming very popular and can be a great source of diversification and "worry free" investing for years to come. After all, as time progresses, these funds will automatically become more conservative, without you doing anything.

Index Mutual Funds

In Chapter 4, we introduced the idea of indices. Specifically, we briefly discussed three of the most well-known indices: the DJIA, the S&P 500®, and the NASDAQ®.

Simply put, index mutual funds attempt to mimic, and subsequently track, a particular index. Although we covered only three of the major indices, there are dozens (if not hundreds) of different indices tracking all parts of our economy and, most likely, a corresponding index mutual fund that tracks that particular index.

Again, as stated, index funds are passively managed. An index fund's mutual fund manager simply selects the same holdings of a particular index and then "lets it ride." There is no real need for a team of analysts researching stocks or bonds in an attempt to find a "hot deal." This means that the expenses associated with an index mutual fund should be relatively lower than actively managed funds.

Mutual Fund Pricing

In Chapter 4, we briefly discussed how the value of a stock can be calculated (i.e., our lemonade stand example). Essentially, the value of a stock can increase or decrease every second during a normal trading day. This means that when you buy a stock you will almost instantaneously see whether it has increased or decreased in value and, subsequently, whether you are making or losing money. Keeping this in mind, a mutual fund is potentially invested in hundreds of different stocks. So, how is the value of a stock mutual fund calculated? An entire book could be written on this subject, so for now, let's try to keep it simple and touch on some main points.

The price per share of a mutual fund is typically represented by, and is commonly called, the NAV (Net Asset Value). In essence, this is the per share price of the mutual fund (i.e., what you would pay to own one share of the mutual fund). The calculation to arrive at the NAV can be quite complicated, but in essence, the NAV is determined by the value of the underlying investments (minus any liabilities) divided by the number of shares outstanding.

For example, let's assume that a mutual fund has invested in the shares of 200 companies, and at the end of the day, the value of the shares of those 200 companies (net of any liabilities) totals $50 million. Additionally, let's assume there are one million shares outstanding. The price per share of the mutual fund (i.e., NAV) would be $50.[15] So, if you invested $5,000 into this fund, you would have 100 shares (i.e., $5,000 divided by $50). But the value of these shares can, and often do, change on a daily basis. For example, let's assume a few days later, the fund's 200 stocks have a net value of $41 million. With one million shares still outstanding, the new NAV would be $41. Your 100 shares would now be valued at $4,100 (a $900-dollar loss). However, the opposite could also be true: the fund's assets could have increased, and a result, you could have made money.

If you were to invest in one stock, you could see the stock's value almost moment by moment throughout the trading day. However, since a mutual fund typically invests in hundreds of different securities, valuing all of them and arriving at a NAV can take some time. An important aspect of mutual fund investing is that you will not know the price (or value) of your mutual fund (i.e., the NAV) until a few hours after the financial markets close because the management team must calculate all the various securities within the mutual fund.

I bring this to your attention because this simple fact, when not known, can create a lot of confusion in the real world. Generally, the price

---

15   Calculation is $50M divided by one million outstanding shares.

of the mutual fund you see during the day is the price of the mutual fund calculated the prior evening. The current day's price will not be known until after the financial markets close, and so if you initiate a liquidation (i.e., sell shares) during the day, you won't actually know what you sell the stocks for until a few hours after the financial markets close. In turbulent market times, this can certainly present some risk, but I wouldn't stress too much on it as the fluctuations generally are not that great. The risk of principal fluctuation (i.e., gains and losses) is still a risk when investing in a mutual fund, but by investing in a mutual fund, you are essentially relying on the investment manager to make worthy investment choices. This presents another risk of mutual funds: *management risk*.

Management Risk

When investing in a mutual fund, you are essentially handing over your money to fund managers who will invest it on your behalf. The types of managers are as varied as the number of mutual funds available for investment. There are fund managers who have Ivy League degrees and others with a wealth of real-world, practical experience. Some fund managers may have been in the business for decades, while other fund managers are new to the scene.

Some managers may have a track record of successfully choosing and managing investments; other managers, perhaps not so much. In fact, from my professional experience, some investors will specifically seek out particular managers and only invest with that manager. This is neither right nor wrong.

Additionally, managers may sometimes decide to retire or leave the industry or accept a new position, and as a result, a new management team may take over the day-to-day functions of a particular fund. This new management team may or may not continue the same sort of analysis as the previous manager. For example, the new management team may assess stocks differently or may have a preference for certain types of companies. Please do not stress too much on analyzing the management team of mutual funds. Although analyzing management teams can sometimes be beneficial for experienced investors, it isn't necessary for those just learning the basics. What's important is knowing that there is management risk when investing in mutual funds.

So, let's briefly recap. A mutual fund is where numerous investors "pool" their monies with a fund manager. The fund manager may specialize in a certain asset class, such as large value stocks or intermediate-term corporate bonds. Whatever the specialty, the "pooled" investor monies usually represents a large amount of capital, such as millions or even billions of dollars. As a result, the fund manager can usually obtain diversification by investing in a variety of companies, in the case of stocks. You will have indirect ownership of the underlying investments, meaning the fund actually owns the individual stocks (or bonds), and you own a proportional share of the fund. The value (NAV) of the fund is determined by the value of the fund's underlying investments, and this value can change moment by moment during regular trading hours. Given the complicated calculations required, you will not know the closing price of your mutual fund until a few hours after the markets close.

It is expected that the fund manager will then continue to monitor the investments and make changes as deemed appropriate. Essentially, the responsibility of analyzing specific companies, making investment choices, and maintaining ongoing analysis is off your shoulders and is now the responsibility of the fund manager.

Think of the costs associated with this responsibility. There may be a need to hire research analysts to help in security selection, maintain an office staff and/or office building, send statements to clients, and a whole slew of other costs. As a result, it should be expected that certain *fees* may be assessed so that the fund manager is paid to cover these costs as well as earn a salary. After all, fund management is a job.

Fees & Loads

The fees associated with mutual funds can sometimes be complex. We will attempt to cover some of the basics. But first, let's discuss how mutual funds are usually purchased and sold. Remember that a mutual fund is essentially an investment manager with whom you and other investors are "pooling" your monies. So, how do you actually deposit your monies with this investment manager?

For some mutual funds, you can go directly to the mutual fund company (usually online through its website) and invest directly with the fund managers. From my experience, a good example of this is Vanguard®. You will usually have to open an account, which normally requires providing personal and financial information (name, social security number (usually for tax reporting purposes as well as Patriot Act verification), investment experience, etc.) and may require an initial deposit (e.g., $2,000) or no initial deposit amount if you "promise" to make monthly contributions.

Once opened, you usually simply pick the fund you want to invest in and your money is invested into that fund. Selling your mutual fund shares is typically just as easy. Another way for you to purchase mutual fund shares is through an intermediary, such as a financial advisor. If you are working with a financial advisor who recommends a certain mutual fund for you to invest in, your financial advisor will usually be able to make the purchase and sell on your behalf. Keep in mind, your personal financial advisor is different than the mutual fund manager. Since your financial advisor is providing you with a service, he/she can sometimes expect you to pay a commission. With a mutual fund, this commission can go by different names but is most commonly called *sales charge* and *load*.

Regardless of whether you use an intermediary to purchase mutual fund shares or work directly with the mutual fund company on your own, mutual fund fees are usually born through two forms: *Loads* and an *Expense Ratio*.

Loads – "Commissions"

The load is essentially the commission you can expect to pay when you work with an intermediary who purchases mutual fund shares on your behalf. A common example of this is when working with a financial advisor. Financial advisors are hopefully providing you with a service, such as recommending an asset allocation, assisting you with budgeting, and other financial planning. When a financial advisor recommends a mutual fund to you and then purchases shares of that mutual fund for you, on your behalf, the financial advisor usually receives a commission. This is part of how financial advisors make a living. We will discuss some of the most common forms of mutual fund loads, or commissions.

Front-End Load – Class A Shares

A front-end load (i.e., Class A) is a commission charged up front when you make a mutual fund purchase. There are numerous regulations that surround mutual fund charges and, in particular, how much a mutual fund load can be. A front-end load charge can range anywhere up to 8%. What does this mean though?

In essence, when you invest in a front-end load mutual fund, you are almost immediately losing money. For example, let's assume you invest $5,000 into a 4% front-end load mutual fund. The front-end load would equate to $200 ($5,000 x 4%), leaving you with $4,800 being invested into the fund. You can consider it a trade-off. Yes, in essence, you are immediately losing money, but hopefully, the service your financial advisor is providing you makes up for that loss. You are essentially paying for the expertise your financial professional provides.

One interesting note about Class A share mutual funds relates to break-points. In essence, the more money you invest into the mutual fund, the lower the potential sales charge. Whereas you might invest $10,000 and be assessed a 5% load, if you were to invest $25,000 that load might be lowered to 3%. These are purely hypothetical figures, but the fact remains you might be able to save on commission charges the more you invest in a particular mutual fund. Always check with your financial advisor or directly with the mutual fund company for the specifics.

Back-End Load – Class B Shares

A back-end load is essentially the reverse of a front-end load; a back-end load usually isn't charged unless and until you sell shares. So, you won't necessarily lose money right away when you invest, but you will when you sell. For example, let's assume you invested $10,000 into the

ABC Large-Cap Value Fund, which has a 4% back-end load (i.e., Class B). First, since this is a Class B share mutual fund, your full $10,000 will be used to purchase shares, but what happens when you decide to sell those same shares?

Let's assume that after two years your fund has increased in value to $12,000, and you decide to sell all of it. The back-end load might then be assessed at $480 ($12,000 x 4%) leaving you with $11,520. Now, some back-end loaded funds may decrease the amount of the charge the longer you hold the fund, but you should expect to pay some sort of load when you sell the mutual fund's shares. Keep in mind, you may pay the back-end load whether you made or lost money. For example, let's assume that instead of increasing to $12,000, your initial investment declined to $8,000 and you decided to sell all your shares. A 4% back-end load could be assessed, leaving you with $7,680.

No-Load Mutual Funds

A no-load fund is just that: it charges no load. Whether you buy or sell a no-load mutual fund, you should not be expected to pay any commission (i.e., load) up front or on the back end. As you can imagine, some financial advisors would not recommend these types of funds to their clients because they would be missing out on a commission. As a result, to purchase no-load funds, you will usually need to open an account directly with the no-load mutual fund company and then make your own investment choices.

Perhaps you are an investor who likes to do your own research and make your own investment choices. You may not need the assistance of a financial advisor and so you want to avoid paying any loads. In this instance, no-load funds may play an important part in your investment portfolio. Loads can be somewhat confusing, and so we will attempt to keep it simple. Essentially, you shouldn't be investing in a mutual fund that charges a load unless you are working with an intermediary who is providing you some sort of service, such as a financial advisor

Expense Ratio

Another fee associated with mutual funds is the *expense ratio*, which is often charged regardless of whether the fund is load or no-load.

The expense ratio is the percentage of assets deducted for ongoing fund expenses. These expenses can include management fees, administrative fees, operating costs, and 12b-1 fees,[16] as well as any other costs the mutual fund may incur. Unlike the load (which is typically paid to the financial advisor or broker), the expense ratio is seen in every mutual fund because the expense ratio is essentially how the fund manager is able to keep the fund operating (e.g., paying bills, salary, costs associated with trading securities). Keep in mind, the expense ratio is usually deducted from the fund's earnings, which means your earnings decrease as a result.

Lastly, to discourage short-term and speculative investors, some mutual funds may charge a *redemption fee*. This redemption fee may apply to both load and no-load funds. The general thinking is that an investor purchasing shares of a mutual fund and then selling those shares short-term creates costs for the mutual fund and may have a negative impact on the fund's performance and for longer term investors participating in the fund. Essentially, if you were to sell your shares within a certain amount of time, a redemption fee may be assessed. You might expect these fees to range between 0.25% and 1%.

Now that we have covered the necessary, but often dreary, topic of fees, let's touch on some high-level concepts of mutual funds. You now know that at its base, a mutual fund can be considered a pooled amount of monies, usually by many investors (hundreds or even thousands) that is then managed by a fund manager. Recalling our three buckets (i.e., three asset classes), we can now deduce that mutual funds will be cash mutual funds (i.e., money market mutual funds, which we covered in Chapter 2), bond mutual funds, or stock mutual funds.

---

16   A 12b-1 fee is an annual marketing or distribution fee on a mutual fund.

ETF (Exchange-Traded Funds)

Modern mutual funds have been in existence for almost 100 years; the first modern mutual fund appeared sometime in the 1920s. ETFs have been in existence since the early 1990s (just about twenty years). As a result, the variety of ETFs, when compared to mutual funds, is quite limited, but they have become a popular investment vehicle.

From one fund in 1993, the ETF market grew to 102 funds in 2002 and nearly 1,000 by the end of 2009.

www.investopedia.com

An ETF acts like a mutual fund. When investing in an ETF, you are choosing to have a management team invest funds on your behalf. The management team will choose the investments and handle the day-to-day operations of the ETF, including buying and selling individual securities, keeping records, and a host of other activities. Also, just like with mutual funds, there are cash ETFs, bond ETFs, and stock ETFs. Essentially, ETFs are mutual funds, except they trade like a stock. What does this mean?

Recall that a mutual fund could potentially have hundreds of individual securities it has invested your money in. As a result, we will not know the value of a mutual fund until a few hours after the financial markets have closed because calculations have to be run to determine the value of all the different holdings within the mutual fund.

However, with an ETF, these calculations are done in real-time, throughout the day. This means that you will know second-by-second the value of your ETF. No more waiting for a few hours to see at what price you bought or sold your fund. With ETFs, you will know almost instantaneously.

Another important aspect of ETFs is that they generally mimic various indices. Instead of having the ability to invest in whatever stocks the management team chooses (as is the case with most mutual funds), ETFs usually invest in the same securities that a particular index tracks. For example, an ETF called the Large Value ETF may track a large value index, such as the Dow Jones Industrial Average (DJIA). The management team, for the most part, is passively managing your money, which means that the management team is not necessarily analyzing various securities throughout the day and making decisions on which individual securities to buy (e.g., stocks). Instead, the management team looks at what securities the index is tracking and then invests in those same securities. Often times, the securities tracked by a particular index stay constant, in some instances for many years or even decades.

Given this passive management, the fees charged on ETFs are generally lower than mutual funds. This should make sense since the management team is simply mirroring an index and not having to make a lot of complex investment choices. Also, ETFs are traded like stocks, which means that they do not charge loads, but instead will usually have commission charges that can be seen with stock trading.[17]

All in all, ETFs are becoming a popular investment vehicle. Just like mutual funds, there can be cash ETFs, bond ETFs, and stock ETFs.

Summary

Mutual funds have been around for quite some time, a century or two (if not longer), but were usually the privy of the wealthy in society. However, with the advent of the modern mutual fund (sometime in the early 20th century), mutual funds have exponentially gained in popularity.

Mutual funds provide investors with the ability to obtain broad diversification and professional money management. A mutual fund is simply a pooled pot of investor monies. There could be hundreds of thousands of investors contributing money into the same mutual fund, which could in turn equate to a large sum of money (e.g., millions or even billions). When you contribute to this mutual fund, you own a proportional share of the overall pot. Essentially, you own what you put in.

---

17   More on commissions in Chapter 12.

One benefit of a mutual fund is that the large pot of money will be dispersed amongst a variety of investments, which in turn provides you with diversification. If you were to invest $5,000 on your own, you may be able to invest in one or two stocks, but by investing in a mutual fund, that same $5,000 will be spread out amongst potentially dozens or even hundreds of different stocks.

How many of us have the time to analyze thousands of companies' stocks and bonds just to determine a handful to invest in? Mutual funds are usually run by professional money managers (i.e., the mutual fund management team) who will engage in a host of activities on your behalf. First will be the selection of what investments to purchase and then ongoing monitoring of those investments and making changes as needed.

Other management team roles can include activities such as providing you services, like online account access, tax reporting and documentation, and record keeping of your investment transactions, as well as helping you purchase and liquidate (or redeem) shares of the fund.

Of course, with these services come fees. After all, the management team needs to make a living and cover the costs of running the mutual funds on a day-to-day basis. The most common fee is called an *expense ratio*. You do not actually pay this fee or even really see it. The expense ratio is usually deducted directly from the pot of pooled investor monies.

Other fees that may be assessed when investing in mutual funds are called *loads,* or *commissions*. Generally speaking, loads should only be assessed if you are obtaining the assistance of a middleman (e.g., a financial advisor) who purchases the mutual fund on your behalf. If you are not using an intermediary and instead are purchasing mutual funds directly from the mutual fund company, then you should be paying no commissions. These types of mutual funds are called *no-load* mutual funds.

Lastly, and this should come as no surprise, mutual funds will be classified as either cash mutual funds, bond mutual funds, or stock mutual funds. For example, there might be bond mutual funds that focus solely on purchasing intermediate-term corporate bonds. There might be stock mutual funds that focus solely on large-cap value stocks.

Additionally, there are asset allocation mutual funds, which attempt to obtain an appropriate mixture of cash, bonds, and stocks all within one mutual fund. There are also asset allocation mutual funds, usually called *aged-based* mutual funds, that will automatically become more conservative (i.e., fewer stocks and more bond and cash exposure) over time, as a certain date approaches (e.g., 2045).

Chapter 7

Creating an Investment Portfolio (Asset Allocation & Diversification)

So now that you know all about the buckets (asset classes), you're probably wondering how this information is actually going to help you build your investments.

Simply put, asset allocation describes the extent to which you invest your money into one or more asset classes (i.e., buckets). In business school, I learned a trick that can help you when reading financial and business-focused material—read phrases backwards. For example, if I take asset allocation and read it backwards, it will read *allocation of assets*. That is to say, how I disburse (allocate) my money amongst the buckets (assets). This is all asset allocation is, determining how much of your money you will allocate amongst the three asset classes.

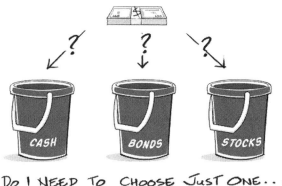

DO I NEED TO CHOOSE JUST ONE...

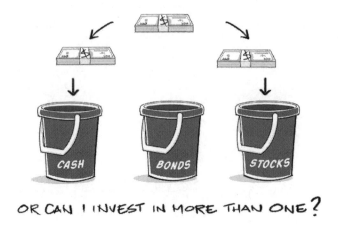

OR CAN I INVEST IN MORE THAN ONE?

Well, of course you can choose to distribute your money however you want—perhaps you invest 50% of your assets in cash and the remaining 50% in stocks. But what is the best choice for you? The answer to this question can have a substantial impact on whether you grow your money, or not. Let's start to make sense of how you can do this, give you some options to consider, and ultimately help you down the road of successful investing.

Asset allocation has been studied and theories abound in the financial world. It is considered by some to be of utmost importance. Getting it right may dictate whether or not our goals are met. So, which factors determine how you should allocate your assets? Time horizon, acceptable risk, and your financial goals. Let's discuss some of the basics of these factors and then tie it all in with asset allocation.

Time Horizon

Just as the name implies, time horizon describes the length of time you will be able to invest your money before you anticipate having to access it. Of course, life events may dictate a different approach, but we really need to try to hone in on the amount of time that we can essentially forget about the invested money. For example, let's assume that you are saving $200 per month for the next two years at which point you will use the invested money as a down payment on a new vehicle. Your time horizon in this instance is two years. Could an emergency occur that requires you to need access to that money before the two years? Of course, but assuming no emergencies, your time horizon is two years.

If you have amassed $10,000 for a down payment on a home, but you do not anticipate buying the home for five years. Your time horizon would then be five years.

Your time horizons can be varied and dependent upon your unique situation, but knowing what your general timeline is for your money can help you make better decisions about how to invest it.

One "rule of thumb" we in the finance profession sometimes use is as follows: cash investments are usually appropriate for time horizons of one year or less, bonds might be appropriate for one year up to five years, and time horizons in excess of five years, you should consider investing in stocks.

You may be wondering why there are certain time periods applied to certain asset classes. I left a few hints in the first couple of chapters, but let's get into more detail now.

As you know, risk is essentially how much the value of an investment fluctuates over time. For example, over a year, stocks can drop quite a lot, but then go back up and even higher the next year. So, if you were investing over a short term, you would avoid stocks because when it comes time to access your money, your stocks could have dropped significantly and you could lose money.

Along the same lines, if you have a long time horizon, let's say it's 10 years, you could put all your money into cash investments, but their lower risk (or chance of fluctuation) means your return will be lower. So, over 10 years, you might end up with about the same amount of money as you started with, which would be significantly less than what you would have had if you'd invested in stocks.

So, if you are saving $200 per month for two years, at which point you anticipate using that money for a down payment on a new car, you will more than likely want to consider a cash type investment. The risk of losing some of your money while in a cash investment is minimal. You have good reason to believe that your money will be there for you in two years, when you arrive at the dealership.

What if you choose to invest in stocks instead? Could stocks also go up over those same two years and subsequently, would your investment have increased substantially? Perhaps. These are some the of risk/reward tradeoffs. Some of us may be willing to take on the risk of losing all of our investment with the hopes of increasing it substantially. However, these "rules of thumb" have some basis in historical return figures for the various asset classes, and a time frame of under five years generally means you will want to avoid stock investing.

To expound on this idea a bit further, let's imagine a 24-year old is saving for her retirement and puts away $100 every month until age 65. The time horizon for this individual is in excess of 40 years. Such a large expanse of time could indicate that she has the ability to assume the risk and potential reward of stocks. Over a course of 40 years, chances are that stocks will show a much greater return than bonds or cash investments. So while stocks can fluctuate greatly on a daily basis, this specific investor doesn't need to worry about the day-to-day, or even year-to-year fluctuations, because she won't be taking her money out for 40 years.

Over the years I have attempted to formulate ways of presenting our rules of thumb in an easy to understand example that will further help us make sense of this investing thing. One of the most effective examples I have come up with relates our investments to that of traveling down a freeway.

The Freeway

I want you to think of a three lane highway. The far left lane is the fast lane, which will be representative of stocks. In the fast lane, we may have the ability to travel at great speeds ensuring that we'll arrive at our destination quicker. However, traveling at such high speeds also poses great risks. Sure, we may arrive at our destination before anyone else, but we are also going extremely fast and if an accident occurs, it could be detrimental to our wellbeing. That is to say that when investing in stocks, we may potentially grow our money much faster when compared to the other asset classes, but if the stock market has difficult times, we may experience substantial losses.

As we shift into the middle lane, represented by bonds, our speed starts to decrease. We are still going pretty fast, but we may not arrive at our destination as quickly as those in the fast lane. However, if an accident occurs, we may not be in as much of a mess as those in the fast lane. The potential losses on bond investing are greatly reduced when compared to stock investing, yet earn potentially higher amounts of interest over cash investments, but again, with more risk. Sort of the "middle of the road" investment.

Finally, when we shift into the far right lane, represented as cash, we have entered the slow lane. When we are in the slow lane, we don't worry about how quickly we will arrive at our destination. The fact that those in the fast lane are zooming past us isn't important. Our main goal in the slow lane is to take our time, enjoy the ride, and get to our destination in one piece. This means that cash investments do not generally grow assets, but instead preserve them.

You need to define how aggressive or conservative you want your portfolio to be based on your goals, risk level and time horizon. Generally speaking, each of us will have our own, unique views on how much risk we are willing to take. However, we can generalize that the longer our *time horizon*, the more risk we will able to accept. For example, let's imagine a 25-year old saving for retirement through a 401(k) with their employer. Our investor plans on retiring in 30 years at the age of 65. Given that this investor has a 30-year time horizon, she should be able to invest a good portion of her assets into stocks.

After all, there is the potential for substantial growth of her assets over that lengthy amount of time, and even if there are "problems" within the stock market, she should have plenty of time to recover and continue on the course. On this same note, the closer to retirement that our investor becomes, she will probably want to consider shifting more of her assets out of stock investing and start to incorporate more bonds into the picture. This is not to say that she will eliminate any stock investments, rather, she will want to consider limiting her stock exposure by selling some of the stocks and investing that money into bonds.

And what about our investor once she enters retirement, what then? At this point in our investor's life, she more than likely is no longer working and will now rely, in large part, on her investments to generate supplemental income. In retirement, since we are usually no longer working and receiving a paycheck, we will rely to some extent on our investments to provide us income. As we learned in prior chapters, bond mutual funds, as well as money market mutual funds (i.e., cash investments), usually provide this sort of supplemental income on a monthly basis. As a result, our investor's portfolio will most likely see even further reduction in stock investments and greater investments within bonds as well as the increasing of cash investments. Again, it would most likely not be wise for our investor to eliminate her stock exposure entirely, but we are simply engaging in tactical shifts of our asset allocation to reflect our goal, and in retirement a common goal is to use the monies we have saved over the last few decades to sustain our way of life. In fact, keeping at least some portion of her investment portfolio in stock investments may help ensure that her investment portfolio grows over time.

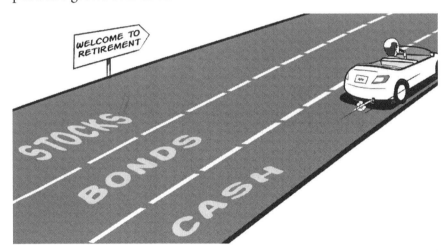

One reason for this "lane change" might be that by staying in the fast lane, our investor may not have enough time to recover from a crash (e.g., stock market crash). For example, let's assume our investor is now 50 years old and entering the waning years of their career, expecting to retire in 15 years. By keeping a large portion of their retirement monies invested in stocks, they are exposed to too much risk. Sure, they are also exposed to the potential for great returns, but what would happen if the economy enters a prolonged recession or worse yet, depression?

All in all, the longer time horizon you have, the more risk you may be able to weather, but how much risk are you willing to accept? That leads us to our next topic: risk level.

Risk Level

Another important factor that can help you determine your asset allocation is your risk level, or how much risk you are willing to take on. We briefly touched on this important topic already, but in a different context. Now, let's expand on it.

Often, risk level can be difficult to define and each individual may have a different level of risk they are willing to accept. For example, if you are saving $200 every month for the next year to go on a vacation, even though your time horizon would suggest we focus on cash investments, you may be comfortable accepting the risks posed by stocks. That is, you might be comfortable with the risk that you may lose all of your investment, because you are willing to "bet the odds" and benefit from a higher payout. You're willing to take on the risk in hopes of having an even better vacation than you could have imagined, but you are also aware and willing to accept the fact that if the stock market heads south, you may not have a vacation at all.

Now what about the 24-year-old who is saving for retirement? Again, the time horizon might dictate that since the investor has over 40 years before needing the money, they should consider at least a portion of their asset allocation (if not most of it) be invested in stocks. However, this individual may not want to invest in the stock market for a number of reasons. Perhaps she witnessed the Great Recession of 2008 and this scared her away from stocks. Perhaps she has heard horror stories of family members losing retirement savings in the stock market. Whatever the experiences, this investor may be determined that the stock market is not right for her, so she opts for lower return, but less risky bond and cash investments instead.

To some, the above examples may seem farfetched, but they are not. In fact, the two examples above are similar to two clients I once worked with. I still remember them to this day. They were both females, one was in her 80s and in retirement. The other in her early 20s in a new and flourishing career, and she was just starting to save for retirement through her company 401(k). Two polar opposites as far as time horizon, and as you will see, risk level.

As I do with all my clients, I attempted to educate both of them on the basics of investing. Once they had a basic understanding of investments, I proceeded to recommend asset allocations to them. Although I don't remember the particular goals of the 80-year-old woman, I do remember that I was leaning towards an asset allocation that was heavily focused on cash investments with a mixture of bonds and perhaps very small percentage of assets in stocks. After all, given her age, her time horizon may be somewhat limited. She would not have it. She had "been around the block" and was quite familiar with the risks associated with stock investing and she was adamant that she wanted to assume that risk. Her risk level would be considered as *aggressive*.

In a similar surprising twist, the woman in her early 20s saving for retirement (with a time horizon in excess of 40 years) did not want any stock market exposure. I remember that I spent quite a bit of time trying to persuade her to consider investing a portion of her money, however small, into stocks. I also remember that she was adamant that she not have any exposure to stocks. Even though other investments (cash and bonds) may not provide the potential growth that stocks can, her risk level dictated a more *conservative* approach to investing.

Goals	Description
Conservative	An investment strategy that seeks to preserve the value of a portfolio by investing in lower risk securities.
Aggressive	An investment strategy that seeks to maximize the value of a portfolio by investing in higher risk securities.

Risk level is a rather personal decision and one that you must determine for yourself. As presented in the above examples, just because you might have a timeframe of years or decades might not mean you will be willing to accept a lot of risk. One rather noteworthy aspect of risk level that you will want to consider for yourself is "*volatility*." For example, certain investments, such as stocks, have the potential for dramatic increase and decrease in value over a very short period of time – the same day in many instances. This increase and decrease in value is what we call *volatility*. For example, perhaps you invest $5,000 into a stock and the next day the value dropped to $4,000 (a 20% decrease). Yet, the very next day or even that same day, your investment could go up in value to $5,500 (a 10% increase). Could you stomach this sort of volatility? If not, then you may want to consider limiting (not *eliminating*) your exposure to stock investments.

If you're having a difficult time figuring out how much risk you can handle, there are numerous free resources online that will tell you the potential volatility of each asset class over a given period of time. Some of these tools will even provide hypothetical illustrations of what you can expect to earn and what your losses could be over a given time frame. From my experience, these types of illustrated calculations tend to shed new light on risk level and help a good majority of us to better define the level of risk we are willing to accept. For the time being, I would like to present to you the below illustration.

RISK LEVEL

CONSERVATIVE ⟶ AGGRESSIVE

Goals

Goals are another important factor you will need to consider when deciding on your asset allocation. For simplicity's sake, we will divide goals into four categories: *preservation, income, growth,* and *speculation*.

CREATING AN INVESTMENT PORTFOLIO (ASSET ALLOCATION & DIVERSIFICATION)

-Preservation-

The main goal of preservation of principal is to maintain your investment balance. Essentially, you want to put your money somewhere safe where you don't want or need it to grow, you simply want to have all of your money there when you need to access it. A common example of this could be a checking or savings account.

When you deposit money into a checking or savings account, you do not expect to see your deposit decline in value, unless of course, you withdraw money. As mentioned in Chapter 2, these types of investments generally fall within the cash bucket and as a result, you should not expect to make a lot of interest. For those of us that have experience with these types of accounts, we are probably all too familiar with the rather infinitesimal amount of interest we earn. This lower amount of interest is the tradeoff we make to ensure that our money is being preserved.

-Income-

Income is another goal that investors may have and from my professional experience, the goal of income is most commonly associated with retirees. For those of us not yet retired, our income is, in large part, based on the paycheck we receive from our jobs. It would be nice to have investments pre-retirement, that could provide supplemental income, but generally speaking, in order to provide a sustainable income stream from investments, we need to have a rather large amount of money to invest. Retirees have usually spent decades creating such a nest egg and now that they are no longer receiving a paycheck, may want that nest egg to work for them by providing some sort of income stream.

One of the most common investments for this sort of income stream are bonds. Remember from Chapter 3 that bonds historically have provided a much larger interest payment when compared to cash investments, but unlike most cash investments, bonds introduce a new level of risk and that is the risk of *principal fluctuation* (think of the teeter-totter).

When interest rates in the economy go up, you can expect your supplemental income in certain bond investments to also increase. This may seem like a good thing and often is, but you must remember that when interest rates go up, even though your income payments may be higher, the value of your bond will most likely decrease. If you do not have any immediate need for the principal amount you invested, then this teeter-tottering of interest rates and bond values should not be too much of a concern. Let me provide you a real-world example of this concept.

A few years back, I was working with a woman in her 80s, who was a retired widow. Over the course of her life, her husband was the one who handled all of their finances. Unfortunately, upon her husband's passing, she was the only one left in charge of her finances and she admittedly had limited knowledge of investments. However, she would diligently review her monthly financial statements trying to make sense of it all and look for any blatant inconsistencies. Her biggest concern surrounded a rather sizeable investment ($800,000) that her husband had made into a bond mutual fund. She knew that each month this particular bond investment would send interest payments directly to their bank account and that those interest payments had been steadily increasing. However, she also noticed that the $800,000 investment was decreasing in value.

One of the first things we did was to clarify what her goals were for this money. Her main objective was income generation. She had no immediate or planned need to actually use the invested amount of $800,000 as they had other assets they could use if need be. Since she didn't need access to the principal value of the bond (the $800,000), I told her she can enjoy the larger monthly interest payment and will have to stomach watching the value of her bond decrease. Equally important was that she understood that interest rates will most likely, at some point in the future, start to decrease and when this happens, the monthly deposits to her bank account should also decrease, but that the value of her bond will increase. This understanding of her bond investment relieved her worries.

-Growth-

Another goal we should consider is *growth*. From my experience working with individuals and their investments, most people want to grow their money. Whether it's money they will be using in six months to pay a child's tuition or money they plan on using for retirement, twenty years away, people always want their money to grow. I get it, I want my money to grow too.

The thing is, as we have learned in the first few chapters of this book, to increase the amount of return you make (i.e., growth), you need to be willing to accept a greater amount of risk and a big part of that risk is that you may lose money. So, for the individual with money set aside for their child's college tuition that is six months away, do you really want to risk losing some or all of it in the stock market in hopes of growing it? For example, let's assume you have $10,000 saved for your child's college tuition due in six months. Would you be comfortable if in six months, when tuition was due, the balance was $7,500? Or would you rather the full $10,000 be there, preserved, when you write the tuition check? On other hand, for the individual that has 40 years until retirement, do you really want to invest your money in a cash account, earning measly interest? That could be the difference between amassing $1 million for retirement versus $250,000. By missing out on the potential growth of riskier investments, you may not have as many assets to fund your retirement.

The answers to these questions may seem obvious to some of us, but keep in mind that each individual needs to determine their own level of risk. Some of us are willing to take more risk than others and that's not good or bad; it just is what it is.

-Speculation-

Speculation is essentially a goal for those of us looking to risk it all in hopes of gaining a substantial amount in return. Speculative investors must be willing to accept loss of their entire invested amount. Rarely have I seen investors with the goal of speculation, except for those investors that are generally wealthy and well-versed in the financial markets. Speculative investments usually require great amounts of initial capital investment, are potentially illiquid, and present extreme amounts of risk along with the potential for great rewards. These types of investments are outside the scope of this book, so why mention them? Well, you will most likely run into this goal throughout your investing life, and it is beneficial to at least have an idea about what it entails.

Table 7.1 Summary of Goals

Goals	Description
Preservation of Principal	An investment strategy designed to preserve capital and prevent loss.
Income	An investment plan that seeks to generate a stream of cash
Growth	An investment strategy focused on the growth of principal.
Speculation	A strategy of taking on significant risk of loss with the chance of a huge gain.

Goals are usually fluid, changing with time. For example, with 20 years before retirement you may have a goal of growth. Usually, a goal of growth indicates the necessity to invest a portion of your money, usually a rather large portion, within stock investments. However, as you near retirement you may want to reduce your risk in exchange for less growth. Essentially, by investing less in stocks and more into bonds and cash, you are reducing the volatility of your money, but at the same time the potential growth afforded by stocks. And once you enter retirement, you may want to have your money start to produce income for you. This may be a time in which you want to see almost no volatility with your money and instead have your money produce income for you. This usually entails large investments within cash and bond investments with minimal investment in stocks. In the preceding example, your goals started off as growth (i.e. pre-retirement) and ended as income (post-retirement). Your goals can and probably will change with time.

Now that we have covered these three very important factors that can help us better define our objectives and as a result, our asset allocation, let's take a look at an example on how we can actually allocate our assets.

Aggressive Asset Allocation & Diversification Example

Let us assume that you have recently left an employer for a new and promising position at another company. As a result, you have decided to rollover your previous 401(k) into an Individual Retirement Account (IRA) in-the-amount of $100,000. Once this money is in the IRA, you will need to determine an appropriate asset allocation. You have determined that retirement is approximately 15 years away (your time horizon) and that you are willing to accept a moderate amount of risk in order to grow your IRA balance (your risk level and goals). You decide on the following asset allocation:

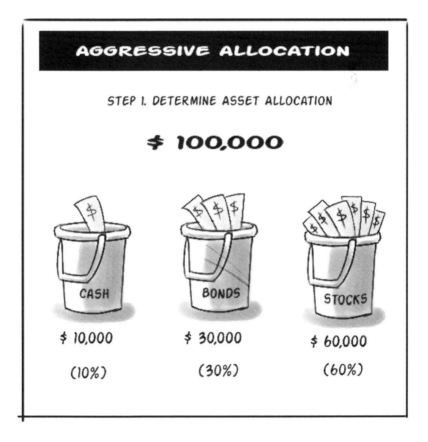

The above illustration provides an example of what the asset allocation might look like for this investor. They have decided to invest a majority of their money into stocks (60%), a more moderate amount into bonds

(30%), and the remaining 10% into cash. As we hinted at earlier, asset allocation is not an all or nothing decision. You do not have to choose all cash or all bonds or all stocks. You can have a mixture of the assets, and in fact, often times this is an appropriate decision to make. In the above example, a good portion (60%) of your money is invested in stocks in hopes of obtaining growth. However, you have also decided to invest the remaining 40% of your money in more conservative investments (cash and bonds). By doing so, some of your assets might be better positioned to weather economic turmoil.

We just discussed one of the first steps in investing and that is deciding on an asset allocation. You can choose whatever asset allocation you like and there really is no right answer, but as we mentioned in our previous discussion, there are some rules of thumb. For example, you can invest all of your money into stocks, or perhaps you will want a little exposure into all three asset classes, or half in cash and half in stocks. The decision is up to you and should be based on your time horizon, the risk you are comfortable with, and your overall goals for your investments.

There are a plethora of theories as to what an appropriate asset allocation is, given your age, time horizon, goals and the like. However, whatever asset allocation you choose, that will not be enough. The next step for you will be to diversify your money within each asset class. While you may know you want to divide your money evenly between all three asset classes, for example, how will that money be allocated within each class? Which types of cash, bond, and stock investments will you put your money into?

Diversification

Once we have determined an asset allocation, we then need to go within each asset class and spread out our money amongst the various investments within each asset class. To illustrate this concept, let's continue with our aggressive investor who decided on an asset allocation of 60% stocks, 30% bonds, and 10% in cash investments.

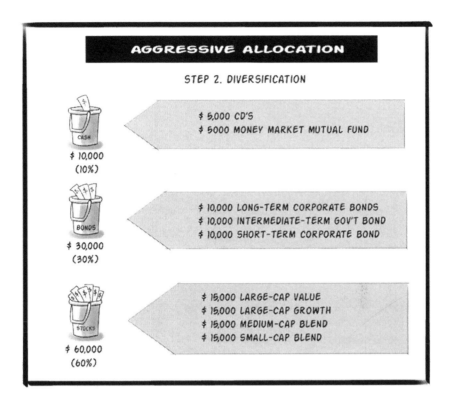

What our investor has now done is diversify her investments within each asset class she chose to invest in. Let's examine what investments she has chosen and why she might have chosen these ones in particular.

Cash Exposure

Our investor indicated that they are looking for growth for their retirement and that they are willing to accept a moderate amount of risk in order to achieve this growth. As we have learned in earlier chapters, growth is mainly reserved for stock and bond investments. Cash, on the other hand, is there to preserve money. As a result, we should expect our investor to have little to no investments within the cash bucket and instead focus on bond and stock investments.

In the example above, our investor has decided to invest only 10% into cash investments. Within the cash bucket, she has decided to diversify her cash holdings evenly between Certificates of Deposit and

Money Market Mutual Funds. The cash investments she has chosen are considered the riskiest of the cash investment options and should provide her higher returns when compared to other less risky, lower-yielding cash investments.

Bond Exposure

When looking at the above bond investments we can see that we have diversification in the form of exposure to long-term corporate bonds, intermediate-term government bonds, and short-term corporate bonds. Referring back to our bond discussion in Chapter 3, corporate bonds are considered to be more aggressive and have more potential for growth and higher interest rates when compared to government bonds. Also, longer term bonds are generally considered riskier when compared to shorter term bonds. After all, with longer term bonds your money is, in theory "tied up" for a longer time.

So, what we see is that she has diversified her bond holdings to include a little bit of each. If interest rates in the economy rise, we can expect her long-term corporate bond value to decrease at a more substantial rate then her short-term corporate bonds, but the long-term corporate bonds should also provide higher interest payments. Her government bond exposure should provide some balance by not being as risky as the other two bond holdings she has. In essence, she is not putting all of her eggs in one basket – the essence of diversification.

Stock Exposure

Our investor has chosen to invest 60% of her overall money into stocks. Instead of investing all of her stock money into just value companies or just growth stocks, she has decided to invest in some value companies as well as some growth stocks. In this way, she's essentially "protecting" her portfolio by playing it safe with some money and putting other money in more lucrative but riskier stocks. What our investor has done is invest a little bit in each so that if the economy starts to perform poorly, she might expect her value stocks to decrease in value less dramatically than her growth companies. Conversely, if the economy moves along at a brisk pace, she would expect her growth stocks to outperform her value stocks.

Additionally, our investor has decided to not only diversify her stock holdings amongst value and growth companies, but also amongst small-, medium-, and large-sized companies. Remember from Chapter 4 that smaller companies tend to provide the potential for more dramatic increases in value, but also more dramatic decreases in value. Once again, our investor is attempting to "protect" her portfolio by playing it "safe" with some money (i.e., large companies) and placing other money in potentially more lucrative investments (i.e., small companies).

The ideas behind asset allocation and diversification are so imperative that I would like to go through another example with you, but this time we will look at a *conservative* investor.

Conservative Asset Allocation & Diversification

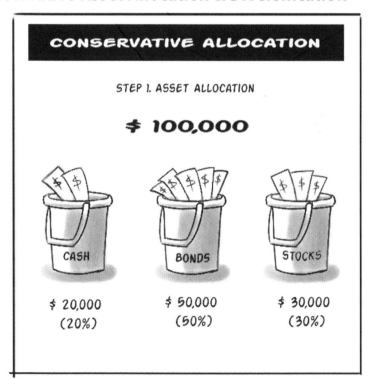

The first thing we can see is that the conservative portfolio is essentially the reverse of the aggressive portfolio. With the aggressive portfolio, our investor had a large portion of her assets in stocks and the remaining amount mixed between bonds and cash. With the conservative portfolio, she has decreased her stock exposure to 30% and increased her bond and cash mixture to 70%. Again, this should be no surprise because bonds are generally considered less risky than stocks, and cash is considered the most conservative of all asset classes. Therefore, by decreasing her stock exposure and increasing her cash and bond exposure, she is coming more in line with what a conservative portfolio might look like. Once again though, our investor must now diversify her holdings. Let's take a look at what that might look like.

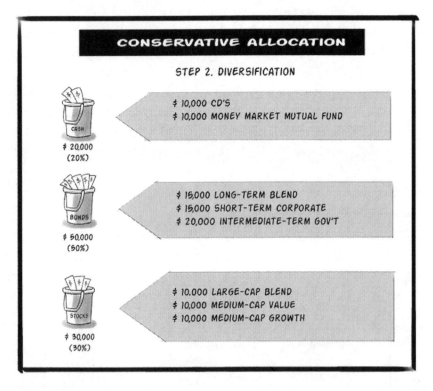

CONSERVATIVE ALLOCATION

STEP 2. DIVERSIFICATION

CASH
$ 20,000
(20%)

$ 10,000 CD'S
$ 10,000 MONEY MARKET MUTUAL FUND

BONDS
$ 50,000
(50%)

$ 15,000 LONG-TERM BLEND
$ 15,000 SHORT-TERM CORPORATE
$ 20,000 INTERMEDIATE-TERM GOV'T

STOCKS
$ 30,000
(30%)

$ 10,000 LARGE-CAP BLEND
$ 10,000 MEDIUM-CAP VALUE
$ 10,000 MEDIUM-CAP GROWTH

Cash Exposure

For the conservative investor, the cash portion of her portfolio has doubled in size from 10% to 20%. Again, cash is usually one of the more "mundane" type of investments that provide investors with a very conservative approach to investment risk. Our investor has kept a 50-50 split between CDs and Money Market Mutual Funds.

Bond Exposure

Perhaps subtle to the untrained eye, yet having a profound impact, is the difference in bond investments. Where our aggressive investor focused mainly on corporate bonds, our conservative investor has focused her bond investments quite heavily into government bonds. She has not eliminated corporate bond exposure, but has heavily decreased it and instead focused on investing in less volatile bond holdings. This might make sense after all, given that government bonds provide more "safety" when compared to corporate bonds.

We learned in Chapter 3 that an important aspect of bond investing relates to the maturity of a particular bond. That is, longer maturity bonds present more volatility whereas short-term maturity bonds pose the least amount of risk. So, what about the maturity of our investor's bond holdings? Whereas in the aggressive portfolio our investor was heavily focused on bond maturities of long- and intermediate-term lengths, she has now flipped this exposure upside down and focuses more heavily on short-term maturity bonds. This means that overall, her bond investments are better positioned and less poised to experience as much volatility during economic ups and downs.

Lastly, our investor's bond holdings have seen a rather dramatic decrease in corporate bond exposure and a rather substantial increase in government bond exposure. Remember, corporate bonds are deemed riskier when compared to government bonds.

Stock Exposure

Our investor's stock exposure in the above conservative portfolio is more heavily weighted toward value stocks as opposed to the aggressive portfolio where we had comparatively more growth stock exposure. This might make sense given that value stocks tend to be representative of companies who produce consumer staples goods and are less reactive to economic conditions (i.e., toilet paper). However, the potential return of these consumer staples, when compared to growth stocks, is rather limited. Our investor is still garnering stock exposure, just with potentially less risky stocks. Nonetheless, our investor has still decided to invest some of her money, albeit a much smaller amount, in growth related companies. By doing so, she is hoping to capitalize on the potentially higher return potential of these growth stocks during good economic times. Yet, by limiting her growth stock exposure, she is also attempting to "protect" her stock portfolio from the potentially dramatic decrease in value posed by growth stocks.

As we discussed prior, another important aspect of stock investing is the size of companies. That is, the smaller a company is, the greater risk it poses for investors both in terms of increasing in value yet also on the downside – decrease in value. What our conservative investor has done, compared to her aggressive portfolio, is to limit her exposure to small companies entirely and instead focus on investing in medium and large size companies.

As a recap, a conservative approach to asset allocation and diversification does not mean that we eliminate exposure to any one asset class (e.g., stocks), but that we might want to focus investing more of our money in the more conservative spectrum of the asset classes. The following image illustrates this point for us.

There are numerous ways to come up with an asset allocation as well as further diversification within the asset categories. You can choose to invest more heavily in value stocks (i.e., toilet paper) rather than growth stocks. You can also choose to invest more heavily into government bonds as opposed to corporate bonds. In both instances, you do not have to eliminate your exposure to the other potentially more lucrative investments, such as growth stocks or corporate bonds, but rather simply limit your exposure to these groups. By doing so, you are bringing your investments more in line with what can be considered a conservative portfolio.

The opposite can also be said for aggressive portfolios. With an aggressive portfolio you may want to increase your exposure to more risky investments such as growth stocks and corporate bonds, but that does not mean you have to "go all in." You can still invest some of your monies in the more conservative investments such as value stocks and government bonds. By doing so, you are attempting to "protect" your overall investment portfolio from the inevitable ebbs and flows of our economy and financial markets.

The overriding point that I would like to stress to you yet again is that determining your asset allocation is not enough. You will need to further diversify your holdings within each bucket to protect your investment and ensure you have a healthy portfolio.

Dollar Cost Averaging

It should come as no surprise that investments can increase and decrease in value over time. In fact, investments, such as stocks, can experience substantial increases and decreases in value during the same day. For many, the goal of investing is to grow our money. When it comes to stocks, this goal can be summed up in the following phrase, "Buy low, sell high." For example, we want to purchase a stock for $10 per share and sell it for $40 per share—or higher! That is one of the ultimate aims of investing in stocks. However, history suggests that the average investor is very good at *buying high* and *selling low* or put another way, losing money. Instead of purchasing a stock for $10 per share and selling it for $40 per share, the average investor purchases the stock for $40 per share and sells it for $10 per share. This is not good except if you are looking to lose money. So, what can you do?

There is a *theory* in finance called *dollar cost averaging*. Let's explain this concept.

Let's imagine that you have $5,000 to invest, and you want to purchase the stock of *ABC Company*, a growth stock. *ABC* is currently trading at $30 per share. If you invest your full $5,000 all at once, you will end up with roughly 166.66 shares. Let's assume that some time has passed and the value of the stock has fluctuated up and down, ultimately closing at roughly $25 per share. At this point, you will have an unrealized loss of $5 per share, or a monetary loss of roughly $834. Again, unless you are intentionally looking to lose money, this is not a good investment outcome.

However, what if instead of investing all $5,000 at once, you were to invest the same dollar amount over a set period of time? For example, instead of investing all $5,000 at once, you decide to invest $1,000 every month for five months. Let's try to visually present this concept.

Table 7.1 – Dollar Cost Average Example

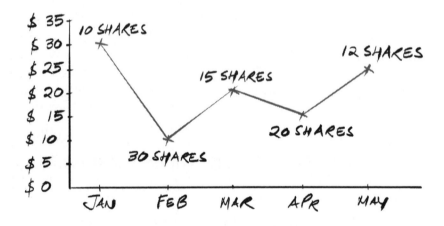

As you can see in Table 12.1, you could have invested the entire $5,000 in January for $30 per share. Again, this equates to roughly 166.67 shares purchased. Now, at that time (i.e., January) you would not have known whether the value of the stock would increase or decrease— again, this is a risk of investing in stocks. The value could have very easily increased in value, but as we see, it did not. So, in May, your 166.67 shares would be valued at $4,166— a loss of almost $900.

Instead of investing all your money at once, you could have easily invested $1,000 per month for five months. Running the calculations, you would have purchased roughly 33.33 shares in January at $30 per share, 100 shares in February at $10 per share, 50 shares in March at $20 per share, 66.67 shares in April at $15 per share and 40 shares in May $25 per share. This means you would have ultimately purchased a total of 290 shares at an average cost per share of $17.24. Thus, even though *ABC* stock ended May at $25 per share (a decrease of $5 per share from the January value), you still would have made money—roughly $7.75 per share.

If you think about it, there are some investment accounts that inherently provide dollar cost averaging. Take 401(k)s for example. We will discuss the particulars of 401(k)s in Chapter 11, but it will bode us well to cover a few brief points as they relate to dollar cost averaging.

When we participate in a 401(k), we usually have a set amount deducted from each paycheck and then deposited into the 401(k). Assuming you have made a proper asset allocation within the 401(k)—again, more on this in Chapter 11—you will be engaging in dollar cost averaging because twice a month (or however often you are paid) money will be invested into certain investments, sometimes purchasing shares when they are high in value, in the middle or low in value.

This is the concept behind dollar cost averaging. Will dollar cost averaging always provide positive results, as in our example? Perhaps not, but it is another tool of investing we can place in our investing arsenal.

The ideas we have been discussing might understandably continue to be confusing for many of us. After all, there is no right answer as to allocate and subsequently diversify your investments

Summary

The idea behind asset allocation is to determine how much of your money you will invest within each asset class. Do you need to invest in all three, just two, or do you want to invest in only one asset class? How well you choose your asset allocation can have a dramatic effect on how well your investments perform and whether or not, in the end, you meet your goals.

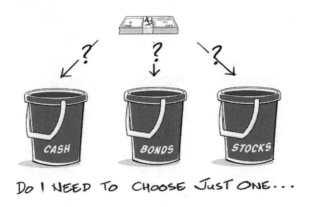

Do I NEED TO CHOOSE JUST ONE...

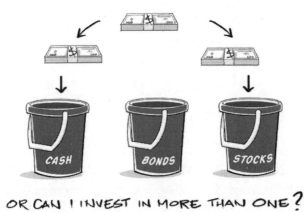

OR CAN I INVEST IN MORE THAN ONE?

Determining your asset allocation doesn't have to be so difficult. In order to help you make sense of it all, I have incorporated quite a few illustrations and tables. These sorts of illustrations have helped many investors decide where and how they will allocate their investment money.

For example, one of the first items on your agenda, when determining asset allocation, is to define your particular goal. The below table lists some of the most common goals as they relate to investing.

Goals	Description
Preservation of Principal	An investment strategy designed to preserve capital and prevent loss in a portfolio.
Income	An investment plan that seeks to generate a stream of cash
Growth	An investment strategy focused on the growth of principal.
Speculation	A strategy of taking on significant risk of loss with the chance of a huge gain.

Often, your goals will dictate which asset classes you should choose. For example, the goal of *preservation of principal* is the most conservative of all the goals with the end game being to keep what you have with little to no exposure to risk. This would probably entail an allocation heavily weighed, if not entirely, into cash. On the other hand, the goal of growth usually entails taking on substantial risk in order to quickly grow your invested amount. This would mean you'd allocate a higher percentage into stocks.

Defining our risk level will further help us determine our asset allocation. The below illustration helps us define which asset class is appropriate for which risk level.

RISK LEVEL

CONSERVATIVE ⟶ AGGRESSIVE

Generally speaking, the more conservative of an investor you are, the more you will want to focus on cash-type investments. This is not an end-all-be-all rule, but they do apply generally.

I also mentioned the idea of defining your time horizon. Essentially, how long will you be able to leave your investment alone without having to access the money? Your answer to this question may also help you further define your asset allocation. After all, certain investments, such as stocks, may have substantial losses in a short period of time, yet may perform better over the long-term. As a result, the shorter your time horizon, the less risk you should be considering. The below illustration summarizes the general time horizons of the various asset classes.

With all of this said, there are no right or wrong answers to these questions and, ultimately, to your asset allocation. The above guidelines are rooted in academic and professional experiences and as such, have validity. I urge you to peruse the internet in search of asset allocation tools. Many of these tools are provided only to the clients of a particular investment firm, but there are some great free tools as well – you just have to look. One of them is on BankRate.com, which after entering some basic investment information, will provide you an idea as to how much you should invest in cash, bonds, and/or stocks. Another free online tool is on Surepayroll.com. This tool is very similar to the BankRate.com tool with the exception that Surepayroll will actually break down not only how much you should consider investing in cash, bonds, and/or stocks (what we refer to as *asset allocation*), but will also provide you with ideas on *diversification*. That is, how much of your stock investments you should consider in large, medium, or small companies and the same with bond investments, corporate versus government.

The concept of "*diversification*" is an imperative aspect of creating an investment portfolio. Once we have decided on an asset allocation, we then need to diversify our holdings within each asset class. For example, within stocks we may want to invest some of our money in growth stocks and other money in value stocks. For those of us that are more aggressive, we may choose to invest only in growth stocks. For our bond investments we may consider purchasing some junk bonds in addition to government bonds. Again, there are no perfect answer for what constitutes proper diversification. What works for Jane may not work for Joe. However, the free asset allocation and diversification tools can help you start to hone in on what you think will be a proper asset allocation and diversification for you and, as always, you can reference this book. We will now turn our attention to a topic that is of utmost importance when it comes to investing: the idea of taxation. Not only will the basics of investment taxation further your understanding of the three asset classes, but it will also prepare you for our future discussions on Individual Retirement Accounts (IRAs) and 401(k)s.

Chapter 8

Capital Gains, Dividends, Interest...and TAXES

Now we need to discuss the basics of taxes as they relate to investing. I believe I just heard a collective sigh from all of you! In fact, some of you may have had the urge to defiantly slam this book shut. In all seriousness, understanding some of the basics surrounding taxes and investments is crucial in furthering our knowledge of investments as well as other topics, such as 401(k)s and IRAs. For the sake of this reading, we will attempt to present very basic ideas as to how taxation works in regard to investing. Tax laws can be diverse and are usually ever-changing. Taxes may be applied at a federal level, state level, and local level. Ultimately, before making any investment decision, you will want to consult with a qualified tax advisor.

Let's begin our discussion with a (hopefully) entertaining example. Let's assume that you have just won a $10 million lottery drawing, and you elect a lump sum distribution. Would the full $10 million be deposited into your bank account (assuming you are the one and only winner)? The answer is no, and why is this? Taxes. Taxes on lottery winnings can be quite high and might include both federal and state taxes. So, instead of $10 million, let's assume you net a deposit into your bank account of $5.7 million. Still not a bad deposit, right?

Generally, when we engage in investing, we are hoping to grow our investment, or *earnings*. These *earnings* can be in a few different forms. For example, the intent of cash investments is not to substantially grow your money, but instead preserve it and, in the meantime, provide you with interest payments. For example, if we deposit $1,000 into a checking account, we may see that deposit grow very slowly over time from monthly interest payments. For cash investments, *interest* will be the main form of earnings.

When we discussed bonds, we learned of the substantially higher risks posed by bond investments over cash investments. Because of these risks, the interest paid out by bond investments should be commensurately higher. In addition to interest payments, and unlike cash investments, bond investments also have the potential to provide a *capital gain*. Remember from our discussion on bonds that we may be able to sell our bond at a premium, which means we would receive more back than what we originally invested. This amount is referred to as a *capital gain*. Therefore, bonds can produce not only *interest*, but also *capital gains*.

One of the main goals of investing in stocks is to create a return on your principal amount invested, or *capital gains*. When we invest $1,000 into a stock, we are generally hoping to see that $1,000 increase in value, hopefully quite dramatically, keeping in mind we may also lose a good deal of our investment. For example, if we invested $1,000 into a stock and then sold that stock for $2,000, we would have realized a $1,000 increase in our investment, or a *capital gain*. Realizing these types of capital gains is usually the main purpose of stock investing. However, some stocks, in addition to capital gains, might also provide what are called *dividends*.

Dividends are usually exclusive to stock investments and are not unlike interest payments. Generally, if a company has managed its financial affairs well, it may have an excess of money and decide to "reward" its stock holders by sending them dividend payments. Some stocks are known for providing consistent dividend payments, and these are usually the stocks of mature, value (i.e., toilet paper) type companies. Regardless, you should understand stock investing will usually provide the potential for *capital gains* as well as *dividends*.

Therefore, we have three main sources of investment earnings: *interest*, *dividends*, and *capital gains* (or *capital losses*—more on this in a bit). Let's briefly touch on each of these as they relate to taxation.

Interest

The taxation surrounding interest is usually pretty basic. Above a certain amount of interest earned, let's say $10.00, you may need to report that interest as "income" on your tax returns. This is usually the case with cash investments, such as checking accounts, savings accounts, CDs, and money market mutual funds. If the interest is under a certain amount for the tax reported year (e.g., less than $10.00), you will most likely not have to report it. The same concept generally holds true for bond interest you may receive. Pretty simple, right?

Dividends

Dividends are payments by a company to stockholders above and beyond what the stockholders have already invested. It is my suggestion that you think of a dividend as a form of interest, except dividends are generally only associated with stock investing. Generally, if you receive dividends above a certain amount, you will need to report that amount when filing tax returns.

Unrealized & Realized Capital Gains

Capital gains are generally associated with investing in bonds and stocks, but mainly stocks. One of the main reasons to invest in stocks, besides the potential dividend payments, is to grow your invested amount (your *capital*). There are two types of capital gains, *realized* and *unrealized*. Let's illustrate this point.

Imagine you have purchased a house for $150,000. A year later, you are curious and decide to check the market value of your home, and it has increased in value to $180,000. This difference is a $30,000 capital gain. However, because you have not sold your house for this amount, the $30,000 is an *unrealized capital gain*. Let's assume that a few months later you once again check the value of your home, and it has declined in value to $125,000. You now have a $25,000 capital loss. However, because you have not actually sold your home for this amount, it is a $25,000 *unrealized capital loss*. If you continue living in the house, you may see more swings up and down, but you don't realize a capital gain or loss until you actually sell your house.

UNREALIZED GAIN/LOSS: A PROFIT OR LOSS THAT EXISTS ON PAPER FOR AN INVESTMENT THAT HAS YET TO BE SOLD

The same holds true for investing. For example, you may invest $5,000 into a stock, and the next day it has decreased to $4,800 (a $200 loss). However, you have not technically lost any money, it is an *unrealized capital loss* because you have not sold the shares of your stock investment. The next day, perhaps the value of your stock investment has increased to $5,600 (a $600 gain). However, you have not actually sold it, so it is an *unrealized capital gain*. You do not actually *realize* a gain or loss until you actually sell your investment.

Short- & Long-term Capital Gains

Another important concept surrounding investment taxation is the idea of *short-term capital gains* versus *long-term capital gains*. Let's continue with the same example as above. You have invested $5,000 into a stock, and six months later you sell it for $5,600. You have a $600 *realized capital gain*. First, because we

LONG-TERM CAPITAL GAIN: A GAIN BY THE SALE OR EXCHANGE OF AN ASSET HELD OVER ONE YEAR.

actually sold the stock for more than we bought it, we have a realized capital gain (of $600) and as such, a taxable event. Additionally, because you sold the stock within one year of purchase, this $600 capital gain will be considered a *short-term* capital gain. If you held the stock longer than one year and then sold it, any gains you may have made could be classified as *long-term*. Why does this matter? The current tax code provides favorable tax treatment (i.e., less taxation) for long-term capital gains.

For many us, the idea of taxation on our investment gains is a hard pill to swallow. However, unless the U.S. Congress changes the law, we will continue to

SHORT-TERM CAPITAL GAIN: A GAIN BY THE SALE OR EXCHANGE OF AN ASSET HELD EXACTLY ONE YEAR OR LESS

pay taxes on our investment earnings and, in particular, on capital gains. I usually try to put a positive spin on taxation of capital gains by reminding myself that this means I have actually made money, similar to the lottery example. Sure, you may have only received $5.7 million from a $10 million lottery jackpot, but at least you made money.

Capital Losses

The last concept I want to discuss is that of *capital losses*. Participating in investing entails risk, and one of the biggest risks is that you may lose some of your principal (i.e., the amount you invested). In fact, you could potentially lose all your principal. It is my suggestion that you set your expectations accordingly and realize now that over the course of your investing life, particularly in stocks, you will probably experience losses. We win some, and we lose some.

Let's assume you purchased a stock for $5,000 and then sold it for $4,800. You have realized a $200 capital loss. One potential benefit of capital losses is that the current tax structure allows capital losses to be deducted on our tax return. In fact, some investors will intentionally sell stocks at a loss to take advantage of this deductibility. However, the amount of losses that can be deducted is currently capped out at $3,000 per year.

Cost Basis

Investing can be a good thing, in that we grow our money. On the other hand, as we have just discussed, taxation might also apply, and the U.S. tax code can be quite complicated. One important aspect of investment taxation is *cost basis*. Cost basis is essentially how we, as investors, measure whether we are making or losing money.

Share Specific Identification

For example, let's imagine a stock is trading at $20 per share, and you purchase $1,000 worth of this stock. This would mean you have 50 shares (i.e., $1,000/$20). Let's then assume that a few months after this purchase you decide to invest an additional $1,000, but this time the stock price is trading at $40 per share. This means you would purchase an additional 25 shares (i.e., $1,000/$40). Your account would now hold a total of 75 shares, 50 of which were purchased at $20 per share and the remaining 25 shares purchased at $40 per share.

Let's then assume that sometime later the stock price dropped to $30 per share. Your first 50 shares will show a profit of $10 per share, or $500. Your remaining 25 shares will show a loss of $10 per share, or $250. Overall, your account balance will show an initial investment of $2,000 with a current value of $2,250. Overall, you have an unrealized capital gain of $250. However, 25 of your 75 shares actually have a loss tied to them.

When you decide to sell a portion of your shares, you might actually be able to report those losses instead of the gains. For example, let's assume you needed to generate some cash and so you decide to sell 20 shares. The market price is $30 so if you sell 20 shares you will generate $600. However, we will need to report to the IRS whether or not we made any gains on this investment.

With share specific identification we can choose which shares to report. Perhaps we tell the IRS that the 20 shares we sold were part of the original 50 shares we purchased, which we purchased at $20 per share. This would mean we would report a capital gain of $200. This gain was calculated based on a $10 per share gain (i.e., 20 shares originally purchased at $20 per share then sold for $30 per share for a $10 per share gain). On the other hand, we might decide to report to the IRS that the 20 shares we sold were part of our second purchase of 25 shares that were originally purchased at $40 per share. In this instance, we will report a $10 per share capital loss. That is, we purchased 25 shares at $40 and then sold 20 of those shares for $30, a $10 per share loss.

What we have been discussing is called *Share Specific Identification* cost basis. This method of cost basis reporting can seem perplexing. What I want you to remember is that with Share Specific Identification, you pick which particular purchase you made and match that up to what you sold your investment for. This method of reporting investment gains can provide wide leeway for whether you choose to report gains or losses.

FIFO (First-In, First-Out)

Another way to report cost basis is through the FIFO method. Essentially, the first shares you bought are the shares you will use to report whether you made a gain—*the first shares in are the first shares out.* Using our prior example, let's assume you sold 25 shares when the market price of the stock was at $30 per share. This entails you having netted $750 (i.e., $30 x 25). However, how much of this is a gain or loss?

Since you are using FIFO as your cost basis reporting, you need to find the first shares you purchased and compare them to the 25 shares you just sold. Remember from our prior discussion that you initially purchased 50 shares at $20 per share. These are the shares you will use to compare to your recent sell of 25 shares at $30 per share. Doing some simple arithmetic, you have a total of a $10 per share capital gain, and since you sold 25 shares that equates to a total *realized* capital gain of $250.

LIFO (Last-In, Last-Out)

The final cost basis reporting method is LIFO, or Last-In, First-Out. This means that when you sell an investment, you will compare the total proceeds of that investment to the last shares you bought.

As in the previous example, you have sold 25 shares at $30 per share for a total capital gain of $750. However, this time you will compare the 25 shares you sold to the last shares you purchased, which were 25 shares at $40 per share.

This means that you actually have a $10 per share loss, and since you sold 25 shares that would equate to a capital loss of $250. This amount is substantially less than the amount reported using FIFO

I would suggest you do not get too bogged down in the specifics of cost basis reporting, which can be very confusing, complex and ever-changing. Nonetheless, my goal is to present these topics to you in a broad overview. Once you become involved in investing, you will undoubtedly encounter these topics and you now have a basic understanding.

Summary

The topic of taxes can conjure up feelings of dread for many of us. Not only can taxes be quite complicated (the IRS tax code is over 70,000 pages in length) and ever changing, taxes usually mean losing money. Nevertheless, understanding taxation as it relates to investing, however agonizing it might be, is essential to understanding the basics of investing.

Generally, when we invest money, we are looking to earn money (i.e., a return). However, certain investments have the potential to lose money. If we lose money, it is called a *loss*, and if we make money, it is called a *gain*. There are three main forms of earnings: interest, capital gains, and dividends. It should be expected that if we achieve returns on our money, the IRS will want to tax those earnings.

One of the most important concepts I would like you to remember is the idea behind *realized* and *unrealized capital gains*. If you were to purchase an investment, such as a stock, you may see the value of that investment increase and decrease over time. So, until you actually sell your investment, you do not actually experience that corresponding increase or decrease in value. Think of our fluctuating home values example.

When you own a home, it may decrease or increase in value, but you don't actually realize that increase or decrease until you actually sell your home. The same idea applies to investments, such as stocks.

A final concept is *cost basis*. If you were to purchase an investment for $1,000 and then sell it for $1,500, you would have *realized* a $500 *capital gain*. This would most likely be subject to taxation. However, the IRS provides numerous ways to actually report this cost basis. This can include *FIFO, LIFO,* and *Share Specific Identification*. These are various methods of calculating whether you made or lost money. It would be a good idea to research these topics further and hire a competent tax advisor prior to deciding on a method of tax reporting.

Again, taxes and investing can be quite complicated, and I urge you not to get too bogged down in the nitty gritty. What we have been discussing in this chapter are the basics, and my intent is to at least get you thinking. Should you decide to invest, you will ultimately run into these tax topics, and hopefully, you will have some familiarity and not be blindsided. Additionally, and equally important, is how these taxes can be avoided entirely through certain retirement accounts, such as IRAs (Individual Retirement Accounts) and 401(k)s. Let's start to discuss these accounts.

Chapter 9
Brief Introduction to Retirement Planning

A brief history of how we, as human beings, particularly as Americans, go about our lives may be beneficial now. It should be no surprise that we do not live in a Utopian society in which our general living needs, as well as wants and desires, are provided for. Rather, our wants and even our needs have costs associated with them and most of us, in order to afford our needs and wants, will need to produce income. We generally achieve this through employment. Our employment usually provides us with a paycheck that we then use to meet our basic needs and hopefully enjoy some of our wants.

However, we eventually age and, with this aging process, comes potential difficulties, such as with health (both physical and mental), that may prevent us from continuing our work. Some of us may have great mental and physical health as we age, yet our desires in life change, and we may want to stop working and instead focus on our true passions in life. But if we are no longer working and producing income (i.e., a paycheck), how do we go about retiring from the workforce when our wants and needs still have costs associated with them?

Historically, we have had three forms of retirement planning at our disposal that could produce income or provide the wealth needed in retirement. These include personal savings, pensions, and social security.

Personal Savings

For Americans, personal savings is generally the least reliable way to save money. A new survey suggests that nearly 7 in 10 Americans have only $1,000 or less in their savings accounts.[18] Whether we are conditioned to be consumers or simply like to spend money, simply put, Americans are horrible at saving money. We just don't save.

And when it comes to savings specifically designated toward retirement, we do not fare much better. The Economic Policy Institute analyzed the Federal Reserve's 2013 Survey of Consumer Finance, and the findings should be startling:

- The median working-age couple has saved only $5,000 for their retirement.

- The median age couple in their late 50s or early 60s has saved only $17,000 in a retirement savings account.

- About 43% of working-age families have no retirement savings at all. Among those who are five to 10 years away from retirement, 39% have no retirement savings of their own.

It should be evident to us that personal savings has historically been an almost non-existent part of American retirement planning. For the time being, unless we Americans drastically alter our personal savings, we can essentially eliminate this form of retirement planning as a substantial part of our retirement income. So, what about the other two forms of retirement savings?

Pensions – "30 and out"

Pensions are essentially going the way of the dinosaur, and the youngest of you may have never even heard of a pension. Even still, it will benefit us to spend some time discussing the pension's historical significance as related to retirement planning.

---

18   Survey: 69% Of American Have Less Than $1,000 In Savings, Sep. 23, 2016, www.forbes.com

The gist of an employer pension was that your employer would set aside money into a "pension account" on your behalf with a promise that after a certain number of years worked, your employer would provide you monthly pension checks for the lifetime of your retirement. In fact, there used to be a saying of "30 and out." This usually meant you would work for 30 years at a particular company and then retire. So, if you started working at age 20, you could perhaps retire as early as age 50 with a promised lifetime monthly pension check from your employer. Not only that, but over the course of those 30 years of employment, you had no responsibility to set aside money or manage the pension fund. The responsibility rested with the employer. This sounds pretty good, doesn't it? In theory, this is a great plan for employees but, in reality, major problems developed.

First, the pension benefit one would receive was a promise by the company, not a guarantee. A company is fallible. As discussed in our chapter on stocks, companies can have bad years in which the economy is not doing well and may need to pull back on certain expenses in order to survive the economic environment. Worse yet, some companies may even go bankrupt, and in the event of a bankruptcy, what would happen to the promised pension benefits? Well, let's look at a real-world example. "In 1963, Studebaker terminated its employee pension plan, and more than 4,000 auto workers…lost some or all their promised pension plan benefits."[19]

Pension plans became too expensive for some employers, which led to actions such as a reduction in promised benefit checks and the halting of monthly benefit checks. In some instances, pensions contributed to the company going out of business and, as a result, a total loss of any promised pension benefit payments.

In 1974, the Employee Retirement Income Security Act (ERISA) was passed, and subsequently, the Pension Benefit Guaranty Corporation (PBGC) was established. The PBGC essentially acts as government insurance as it relates to employee pension benefit plans. This is not to say that if a company were to no longer remain a going concern (e.g., go out of business), employees promised pension payments would be

---

19   History of PBGC, www.pbgc.gov

guaranteed in full, but the PBGC would step in to ensure that some sort of payment would be made.

Regardless of this Congressional act, pensions would slowly become obsolete. They essentially became, and are, too expensive for companies to provide. According to a September 15, 2014 article in the *Wall Street Journal*, "Sixty percent of Fortune 500 companies offered defined-benefit pensions to new hires in 1998…By the end of 2013, that portion had dropped to 24%."

It should be clear for a majority of Americans, particularly the younger generations, that employer pension plans will most likely not even be an option for retirement income. For those of you who have employer pensions, good for you, but for those of us who don't, particularly the younger generations, we should not expect to have a pension as a source of retirement income.

So, we Americans essentially have no personal savings set aside for retirement, and we will most likely have no access to pension benefits for retirement. What does that leave us?

Social Security

I realize a discussion surrounding Social Security and worse yet, statistics, may start eyes glazing over, so why do we even need to discuss it? Is it that important?

As the below quotation illustrates, social security will play an important role in many Americans' retirement planning. As a result, I ask that you bear with me as we discuss a brief history surrounding Social Security.

97 percent of Americans age 60-89 either receive benefits today or will receive benefits in the future.

WhiteHouse.gov, August 14, 2015 blog by Jason Furman and Jeffrey Zients

"The Great Depression was clearly a catalyst for the Social Security Act of 1935…to offer immediate relief to families. The Social Security Act was signed by President Franklin D. Roosevelt on August 14, 1935. Taxes were collected for the first time in January 1937 and the first one-time, lump-sum payments were made that same month. Regular ongoing monthly benefits started in January 1940."[20]

Social Security is a program based on contributions that workers make into the system. While you're employed, you pay into Social Security, and you receive benefits when it's your turn to retire. Contributions are the Federal Insurance Contributions Act (FICA) taxes that are withheld from most paychecks.[21] When you work, 85 cents of every Social Security tax dollar you pay goes to a trust fund that pays monthly benefits to current retirees. The other 15 cents goes to a trust fund that pays disability benefits. Social Security was never meant to be the only source of income for people when they retire, and it replaces about 40 percent of an average wage earner's income after retiring.[22]

Although Social Security was not, and is not, intended to be a sole source of retirement income, from my experience, a good majority of Americans rely heavily on monthly social security payments for meeting their retirement income needs. It is probably no surprise to most of us that social security income has some potential issues.

Usually, every election cycle, we are inundated with discourse surrounding Social Security retirement benefits. The dialogue usually includes whether the Social Security Income program will be able to sustain itself over the coming decades and cautions the program may become insolvent, future benefits may be reduced, taxes might be raised, or younger workers may have to work longer before collecting benefits.

Many of these statements are born from political discourse and partisan bickering and may incite unnecessary fear, but the concerns are very real and must be addressed. In fact, the following quote is taken directly from the Social Security website: "the Social Security Board of Trustees projects program costs to rise by 2035 so that taxes will be enough to pay for only 75 percent of scheduled benefits." I

---

20   www.ssa.gov
21   "How does Social Security Work?", www.money.cnn.com
22   2016 Social Security Understanding the Benefits, www.ssa.gov

do not imagine, barring some drastic political actions, social security income will go away completely, but nonetheless, there is uncertainty surrounding the future of social security income payments.

> **Nearly 80 million baby boomers will file for [social security] retirement benefits over the next 20 years – an average of 10,000 per day.**
>
> Social Security Administration Annual Performance Plan for Fiscal Year 2012

The problem, if there is one, seems to be extremely complicated and the solutions equally so. Some solutions being bounced around talk of reducing benefits, raising the age at which future generations can start collecting benefits, and tax policy (e.g., raising taxes). Sure, Social Security is a hotbed topic in the political world, but it can have potentially dire consequences for millions of Americans who currently, or will in the future, rely on Social Security Income as a primary source of retirement income.

We have just discussed three of the main forms of retirement income that we, as Americans, may rely on: personal savings, pensions, and social security. For many of us, at least two of these avenues (i.e., personal savings and pensions) will not be reliable. The third, Social Security, will most likely continue to be a reliable source of income, but has some major challenges facing it, and the benefits provided by the program are not intended to be an end-all-be-all of retirement.

Summary

There will usually come a time in most of our lives in which we will want to retire from the grind of the workforce to pursue our passions in life, whether they be traveling the world, gardening, or, my personal favorite, watching endless episodes of *The Price is Right*.

For some of us, in order to retire from the workforce, we will need to have amassed a small fortune that will last us through our retirement years. The most common forms of this retirement have historically been personal savings, pensions, and social security.

As we learned, Americans are absolutely horrendous at saving, especially for retirement. Unless our spending and savings habits change, personal savings is essentially off the table. What about pensions? Well, the idea behind a pension seems very attractive. Unfortunately, history has shown pensions have become unsustainable and, as a result, are becoming extinct. Once again, pensions are off the table. What does that leave us with? Social security.

Social security will most likely not go away anytime soon, but the rhetoric we hear each election cycle certainly begs the question as to whether changes are coming down the pike. Perhaps the retirement age will be raised, benefits reduced, or taxes increased. We just don't know. Given the uncertainty surrounding Social Security Income benefits we will need to consider other forms of retirement income, but what are some of these "other ways"?

Over the last few decades, two types of retirement accounts have made their way into the fabric of American retirement planning: the Individual Retirement Account (IRA) and the 401(k). Many, if not all of you, have probably had exposure to at least one of these accounts. In fact, many of you probably have both accounts open and active as you read this book.

So, what are these accounts, how do they work, and how might they benefit you?

Chapter 10

Individual Retirement Accounts (IRAs)

IRA stands for individual retirement account and is a widely used retirement investment vehicle that has not only gained incredible popularity but is also becoming a crucial part of American retirement planning. In fact, many of you probably have at least heard of an IRA and perhaps even participate in an IRA or two. However, from my professional experience, a good deal of us do not understand the basics surrounding an IRA. Do you simply deposit money and the IRA is supposed to automatically grow for your retirement? How and why does it grow? Do all IRAs act in the same manner? Let's address the basics of IRAs and find answers to these questions.

When working with clients, I would pose the following question: "Tell me what you know about an IRA. What does it do, and how does it work?" The responses I received were the usual, "Well, it's an account for retirement that I contribute to, and it's supposed to grow over time."

I am not making light of nor mocking the seemingly general lack of knowledge surrounding the basics of investing and, in this case, IRAs. Rather, I hope to make you aware that you are not alone in your potential lack of knowledge surrounding IRAs. Secondly, I want to stress to you the importance of at least learning about the basics. After all, as we will momentarily see, IRAs will most likely be a crucial part of your retirement. With that said, before we delve into the specifics of IRAs, let's briefly discuss the history of the IRA.

Brief History of the Individual Retirement Account (IRA)

In the previous chapter, we discussed the history of and some general ideas surrounding the most common retirement vehicles available to Americans. Some of these retirement accounts, such as employer pensions, are becoming obsolete and forcing us to look at new retirement planning vehicles. For example, we discussed the idea that employer pension plans were once a main source of retirement income for a good majority of Americans, but these plans are disappearing. Without these types of plans, many Americans could face the prospects of delaying retirement (to save more) or having a much more frugal retirement. In an attempt to rectify the situation, Congress passed The Employee Retirement Income Security Act of 1974 and introduced Americans to the Individual Retirement Account (IRA).

There were two goals to this legislation. One goal was to provide a tax-advantaged retirement plan to employees who worked for companies that did not provide pension plans. A second goal was to provide a tax-advantaged retirement savings vehicle that would prompt Americans to save for retirement. By saving for their own retirement, Americans may help avoid a potential financial catastrophe for the U.S. Government.

Although the Individual Retirement Account quickly became a popular investment vehicle, many Americans, particularly the not so well off, were not participating. After all, if we are living paycheck to paycheck, how will we find the money to set aside for retirement? Plus, there were strict rules defining who could contribute to an IRA and how much they could contribute. Over the next several decades, Congress passed numerous reforms that attempted to make investing in an IRA a much simpler process. So, how have these new laws, and the subsequent use of the IRA, fared?

In 1975, the estimated IRA contributions totaled approximately $1.4 billion. Fast forward to 2009, and IRA assets were estimated at approximately $4.3 trillion. Clearly, IRAs have become a popular retirement investment vehicle, and it will benefit you to garner at least a basic working knowledge of how they function. But how do they work?

Basics of an Individual Retirement Account (IRA)

I want you to imagine a big, empty garage with a big door on the front. On the building is written the word "IRA." This is all an IRA is, a big empty account, a "shelter" if you will. Yes, it really is this simple!

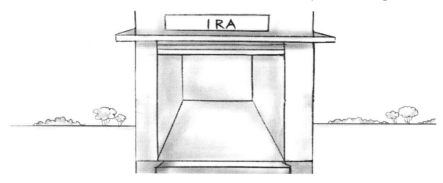

You then can deposit money into the IRA.

Once you deposit money into an IRA, you essentially have a pile of cash, within the IRA, waiting for you to make investment choices.

However, what happens when you deposit money into the IRA? Is the IRA just supposed to automatically invest your money for retirement and hopefully grow in value? Are there investments within the IRA, and if so, what investment choices will you have available to you? It is my hope that by now you are immediately able to answer this last question. After all, what are the three asset classes of investing?

That's right. An IRA is just an account, a shelter for your money, and inside the IRA are various investment choices. You will need to go into your IRA and select which assets you will invest your money into. If this seems daunting, fret not. We spent the first few chapters of this book discussing the foundations of investing; investments will fall into one of three asset classes: cash, bonds, or stocks.

Also, keep in mind the idea of asset allocation, which we devoted Chapter 7 to discussing. That chapter provided insight into how to subsequently invest your money amongst the three asset classes. Remember the freeway? What about your personal preferences for risk tolerance, goals, and time horizon? These are all ideas that will help you determine your appropriate asset allocation. I realize this may seem overwhelming, but I sincerely hope the preceding chapters of this book have at least started you thinking about these topics.

So, these are the basics of an IRA and how it works: it's a big empty "building" that you deposit money into, and once there, you then need to choose which asset classes to invest your money in. How well you invest your money will determine whether your IRA will grow in value and by how much. With that said, there are two types of IRAs as of the publication of this book: Traditional and Roth.

Traditional IRA

Entire books could be written on Individual Retirement Accounts, but for the sake of this introduction, we will focus on what I consider a few key points.

"Tax Sheltering" - No Taxation on Earnings

Remember from our brief introduction into retirement planning that Americans are quite awful at saving. This could potentially create a great burden on our government welfare programs in the future. In order to entice us to start saving, the IRS offers no earnings taxation within an IRA. Thus, one of the main benefits of investing in an IRA is the elimination of capital gains, interest, and dividend taxation.

In Chapter 8 (on taxation), we discussed capital gains. For example, if we invested $1,000 in a stock, and then subsequently sold that stock for $1,500, we would have realized a $500 capital gain. Outside of an IRA account, we would potentially owe capital gains taxes on the $500. Let's assume that capital gains tax rate is 20%. This would mean we really only made $400 because 20% ($100) of the $500 would be paid to the IRS as capital gains taxation.

In an IRA, we do not owe these capital gains taxes (nor interest or dividend taxation). This means that we keep more of our money, and as a result, particularly if we reinvest those gains, we can potentially grow our retirement savings to a much larger amount.

Deductibility & Taxation

Another important feature of a Traditional IRA is the potential ability to deduct your Traditional IRA contributions from your taxes (i.e., a tax deduction). But what does this mean, how does it work, and how could it benefit you?

The IRS has set limits on how much we can contribute to an Individual Retirement Account. As of the writing of this book, the current annual contribution amount (for both a Traditional and Roth IRA) is $5,500 for those of us under age 50 and $6,500 for those of us over age 50. The IRS allows some of us more *seasoned* people to contribute more money based on our age. This is called a *catch-up contribution*. Keep in mind that the annual contribution limit (i.e., $5,500 or $6,500) is for all your IRAs. For example, if you have a Roth and a Traditional, you could contribute 50% to the Roth and 50% to the Traditional (or whatever amount you want). However, you cannot contribute $5,500 to both—the limit is the total amount you can contribute to all your IRAs combined.

The funds you deposit into a Traditional IRA have already been taxed as ordinary income (e.g., through FICA tax on your paycheck). This means that the money you contribute to a Traditional IRA has already been taxed by the IRS. When you file your tax return, you will notify the IRS of your Traditional IRA contribution(s), and this will allow you to then deduct your contribution amount from your taxes. In theory, this means you will "get back" the income tax that was levied on your money.[23]

However, as is seemingly always the case with laws, there is a catch. The IRS has imposed income limitations on whether you can actually deduct your Traditional IRA contribution from your tax return. Think of it this way, if you make a lot of money, the IRS doesn't want to give you a break. If you find yourself in this situation, you could still contribute to the Traditional IRA, you just would not be allowed a tax deduction on the contributed amount. We call these types of contributions to a Traditional IRA "non-deductible contributions." Although you might not be able to obtain a tax deduction, you could still obtain the tax sheltered benefits of investing in and IRA. Whatever happens, whether you make a deductible or non-deductible contribution, it is imperative that you correctly report the contributions on your tax return. Why is this?

Since one of the "benefits" of a Traditional IRA is to provide a tax deduction, in the eyes of the IRS, once you have deducted your contribution from your taxes, that money has now reverted back to being pre-tax (i.e., you essentially receive the payroll tax back upon

---

23   As federal and state tax rules are subject to frequent changes, you should consult with a qualified tax advisor prior to making any investment decision.

claiming the deduction on your tax filing). Do you think the IRS, in the goodness of its heart, will never tax that money?

"In this world nothing can be said to be certain, except death and taxes." ~Benjamin Franklin

When you make a deductible contribution to a Traditional IRA, the IRS will once again levy income tax on that money, but not until you withdraw your money, hopefully many years down the road in retirement. This would be a good idea for those of us who are in a high tax bracket currently and expect to be in a low tax bracket at retirement. For example, John is 36 and is a high-flying lawyer who makes a lot of money, and as a result, is in one of the highest tax brackets, let's say 33%. However, John anticipates that in retirement, because he will no longer be working, he'll be in a lower tax bracket, we will say 20%. John can potentially obtain a tax deduction on his contribution now (essentially, he does not pay the 33% income tax) and instead will pay income tax at the lower rate (i.e., 20%) upon withdrawal in retirement.

Note that if you make a *non-deductible* contribution to a Traditional IRA and do not notify the IRS of this on your tax filing, then when you subsequently withdraw those contributions at a later date, the IRS will not know any better and will levy income tax on the non-deductible amount. In essence, you will then have been taxed twice on the same money—not a good thing for you! For example, let's assume your paycheck (*after* taxes) totals $1,000, and of this amount, you contribute $100 to a Traditional IRA. You then find out that you are unable to deduct this $100 contribution on your tax filing. If you do not notify the IRS that this $100 contribution was non-deductible when you subsequently withdraw it, the IRS will levy income tax on it. Therefore, you will have paid income tax twice on the same money: first, through payroll tax and then on your tax return for the year in which you withdraw the $100. Had you simply notified the IRS that the $100 was non-deductible, you would not have had the *second* levy of taxes. Although our example is only $100, often in the real world, these amounts are in the thousands if not tens of thousands of dollars.

What we have discussed thus far should reaffirm two important points. First, it is imperative you report your Traditional IRA contributions correctly on your tax return. Time and time again, I have worked with clients who have not reported their contributions correctly, and it comes back to bite them in the butt, maybe not right away, maybe not in a year or two, but eventually, perhaps decades down the road. I do not want that to happen to you. Secondly, Traditional IRAs are for those individuals who believe they will be in a lower tax bracket at retirement. However, don't fret too much. Regardless of your eventual tax bracket, saving for your retirement is beneficial.

Traditional IRA Withdrawals

Now, we need to cover a few more specifics surrounding withdrawals of money from a Traditional IRA. The whole idea behind an IRA, and the subsequent benefits of contributing to one (e.g., deductibility, elimination of earnings taxation), is so that you save for retirement. In fact, retirement is in the name: Individual *Retirement* Account.

Typically speaking, we will owe income tax on the money we withdraw from a Traditional IRA (excluding non-deductible contributions), whether we withdraw the money at age 25 or age 75. However, *and please pay attention here*, if you withdraw money from a Traditional IRA before age 59.5, then you may owe a 10% penalty tax in addition to income taxes.

This 10% penalty tax is called an *early withdrawal penalty* (i.e., withdrawing money prior to age 59.5.). Why did the IRS choose age 59.5? I really have no idea; perhaps the age determination was based on actuarial type computations. Without delving too deeply into it, actuarial calculations deal with quantifying and redistributing risk. Whatever the case, and once again, there is a caveat(s) to the 10% early withdrawal penalty.

The IRS will not assess a 10% penalty for an early withdrawal *if* the withdrawn money is used for a particular purpose. What are those particular purposes? The IRS sets the guidelines on what is and is not considered a valid purpose. Some of the current valid purposes are the use of those funds for certain educational expenses, a first-time home purchase, certain medical expenses, and disability. There are a few more reasons, but you should understand all reasons are rather strict.

A point of confusion with many people I have worked with surrounds when Traditional IRA taxation (both the income and penalty taxes) is assessed. Let's assume that you have $10,000 in a Traditional IRA and all your prior contributions were deducted on prior tax returns. Let's also assume that you are 47 and decide to withdraw your entire account balance to go on a vacation of a lifetime.

You will owe income tax and a penalty tax on that money, but you won't pay those taxes when you withdraw the money. In essence, you can access your full $10,000 (minus any fees your financial institution might charge). The surprise for most people usually comes when they file their taxes for that year. Upon your income tax filing, you will then need to pay those taxes, and if you have to pay income tax and a tax penalty, it can add up!

On a final note, age 59.5 is the "magic" age at which you can start to take penalty free withdrawals from a Traditional IRA. Essentially, at or above age 59.5, any withdrawals from a Traditional IRA (excluding properly reported non-deductible contributions) should only be assessed ordinary income tax upon tax filing.

Once again, we are covering some very nitty-gritty topics surrounding taxation as it relates to IRAs, and I wouldn't be surprised if many of you need to take a mental respite. I get it, I really do, but I want to stress that these are the topics most clients I have worked with end up getting confused about. Had they only had a bit of knowledge prior, they would have potentially been relieved of much anxiety.

Roth IRA

The Roth IRA shares almost the same characteristics as that of a Traditional IRA with a few small exceptions. Like a Traditional IRA, a Roth IRA is simply a big empty account, that you contribute money to, and then subsequently invest that money.

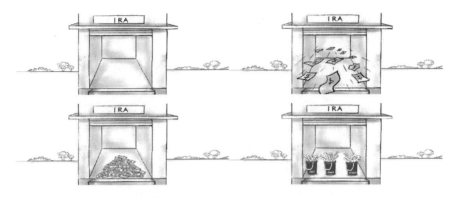

This means that, just like a Traditional IRA, a Roth IRA provides a tax-sheltered account such that taxes on earnings (e.g., capital gains, dividends, and interest) are not assessed while your money is invested within the Roth IRA. Once again, why would this matter to you? Well, you are able to keep more of your money (i.e., not lose it to the IRS in the form of taxes) and hopefully grow it into a much larger amount. The contributions to a Roth IRA are where we start to see some noticeable differences.

First, the money you contribute to a Roth IRA is not allowed to be deducted on your tax return. This means that your contributions (already taxed through FICA payroll taxes) will not be assessed income tax upon withdrawal. This means a Roth IRA is a non-deductible IRA in which you are essentially paying taxes now rather than later. This is an important idea and one that can help you determine which type of IRA to open. For example, let's assume you are in a 20% income tax bracket, but expect that, in retirement, you will be in a higher tax bracket, let's assume 30%. Would you rather pay 20% in income taxes now or 30% in income taxes later? If the former, then a Roth IRA might be a good option for you to consider.

One of the benefits usually touted about Roth IRAs is that upon reaching age 59.5, any withdrawals you take will be tax and penalty free.[24] Also, you can withdraw contributions from a Roth IRA anytime penalty and tax free. These features of Roth IRAs usually garner the most attention and are why many people decide to open Roth IRAs. It

---

24 To be completely tax and penalty free, you will need to have reached age 59.5 and have had the IRA open for at least five years.

sounds amazing to not pay taxes! However, there are a few key points to keep in mind first.

First, just like with a Traditional IRA, the money you contribute to a Roth IRA has already had income tax assessed on it through payroll taxes. This means that since your *contribution(s)* has already had income tax assessed on it, you will not owe income on that money when you withdraw the funds, so you can withdraw your contributions from a Roth IRA whenever you want, even before age 59.5, and you will not owe taxes on that amount, nor will you owe a penalty tax.

Yet again, there is a very important caveat to this notion that many people either overlook or are unaware of: the difference between contributions and earnings. For example, let's imagine you have contributed $5,000 to a Roth IRA and a few years later the account balance has increased in value to $7,000. This means you have contributions totaling $5,000 and earnings totaling $2,000.

At any time, you can withdraw the $5,000 in contributions penalty and tax free. However, if you withdraw any *earnings* prior to age 59.5, you may owe both ordinary income tax and a 10% early withdrawal penalty. Let's go over another brief example to reinforce this point.

Let's assume you have a Roth IRA account balance of $10,000, and of that amount, you contributed $6,000. This means that $4,000 can be attributed to earnings (e.g., capital gains). If you withdrew the entire $10,000, you would not owe tax on the $6,000 because that is the amount you contributed, but you could owe ordinary income and, if withdrawn early, a penalty tax of 10% on the $4,000 of earnings.

One last, yet important, aspect of a Roth IRA is who can contribute. Not everyone can. Once again, the IRS will not allow those of us who are considered "higher earners" to contribute to a Roth IRA. Fret not, if you are one of these "higher earners," you can possibly still make a non-deductible contribution to a Traditional IRA.

At this point, I understandably may have lost many of you. Some of you may have already decided to close this book or your thoughts have drifted to what you will be making for dinner. Tax discussions can run dry rather quickly. However, we have only brushed the surface of tax topics as they relate to investments. Again, an entire book or series of books could be written on taxation, investments, and IRAs. My goal though has been to present to you with some of the basic tax concepts I believe will benefit you in furthering your knowledge of investing and, in this instance, Individual Retirement Accounts. The above taxation topics are what you will most likely encounter when you go out into the investing world. Hopefully, you are now better prepared.

Summary of IRAs

As explained in the prior chapter on retirement planning, IRAs are one of the main sources of retirement savings that Americans have available to them. I would bet my bottom dollar that almost all of us will have one at some point in our lives. With that said, I want you to take away some key points.

One of the first, and in my opinion, most important, aspects of Individual Retirement Accounts is presented in the following illustrations:

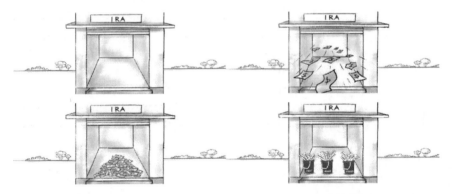

An IRA (both Traditional and Roth) is simply an empty account. That is all they are—a shelter if you will. Assuming you meet IRS limitations (e.g., income, age) you can contribute money into the IRA, at which point you will have a pile of cash. This is the extent of understanding for most clients I have worked with. At this point, many people assume the IRA is an investment in and of itself and should simply grow over time.

However, as you should now know, you actually need to go into your IRA and make investment choices amongst the three main asset classes.

There are a few important tax topics surrounding IRAs that you should be familiar with.

First, both types of IRAs offer the benefit of tax-sheltering earnings (i.e., capital gains, dividends, and interest). This is a potentially massive benefit in that you can keep more of your money, that otherwise would have gone toward taxes, and hopefully grow your retirement savings much more quickly.

Second is the potential for deductibility of contributions into a Traditional IRA. Again, the "higher earners" of our society may not be allowed this benefit but could potentially still make non-deductible contributions to a Traditional IRA.

Last, if you are in a high tax bracket during your earnings years and expect to be in a low tax bracket during your retirement years, a Traditional IRA might make more sense. Again, would you rather pay higher taxes now or lower taxes later? If you anticipate being in a higher tax bracket at retirement, a Roth IRA might be an appropriate option.

The usual benefits touted about Roth IRAs concern the tax-free withdrawals that can be made. Keep in mind, you already paid income tax on the money you contribute to a Roth IRA, so you do not really "avoid" taxation. You simply pay taxes now rather than later. As a result, you can withdraw your contributions from a Roth IRA at any time and at any age, tax and penalty free. However, the earnings in a Roth IRA may have income tax and an early withdrawal penalty assessed to them. To avoid taxation (both income tax and penalty taxes) on your earnings within a Roth IRA, you will need to have reached age 59.5 and have had the Roth IRA opened for at least five years.

Let us now turn our attention to 401(k)s, which as we will see, share many similarities with IRAs.

Chapter 11
401(k)s

The 401(k)

How important is it for you to learn the basics of your 401(k)? Let me share with you a conversation I had with a client a few years back.

She was approximately 63 years of age, single with no kids, had worked in retail for most of her life, and had recently retired. Over the course of her career, she diligently contributed to her company-sponsored 401(k) plan, amassing approximately $200,000, of which roughly $160,000 were her total contributions to the plan (the remaining $40,000 was the investment's growth over a few decades: *earnings*).

When we first started working together, she was understandably frantic as to why her account had not grown much in the past few decades. After all, historical records suggest that certain investments, such as the U.S. stock market, have traditionally provided an average annual return of 10%,[25] and it appeared her account returned low single digits, which was going to have a real effect on the quality of her retirement. After all, like many Americans, her 401(k) was going to be her main source of retirement income (coupled with social security income) and would need to last her a few decades—and it was only $200,000. What about the retirement vacations she had dreamed of taking? The beach house she was looking forward to buying? And what about the

---

25   Source: www.moneychimp.com, S&P 500 returns (dividends included): Robert Shiller and Yahoo! Finance.

necessities of retirement, like food, clothes, and entertainment? All of these were in jeopardy, and unfortunately, some of her retirement dreams would need to be altered.

I assured her we would look at her finances, see what happened, and then attempt to forge a way forward. As with most clients, I started by asking her to describe to me how her 401(k) works. Her response was essentially the following statement: "It's an account for retirement that I contribute money to, and sometimes my employer does as well, and it's supposed to grow." Does this sound familiar to you?

From my personal and professional experience, the above description is the extent of understanding that most people have regarding their 401(k)s. Although the statement is largely true, it drastically understates the intricacies. She was obviously an active participant in her retirement planning, but lacked basic knowledge of investing. When she had signed up for her 401(k), her contributions defaulted to the most conservative investment available within her 401(k). In the 1990s, most employers did not offer free advice when it came to 401(k)s nor did employers automatically default contributions into an "appropriate" investment mix (i.e., asset allocation)–as they often do now. Instead, the responsibility rested and, to a large extent still rests, with you. I explained to her the following.

"I want you to imagine a big empty garage building with a front door. This is all a 401(k) is, a big empty account—a shelter, if you will—for your retirement money. Every so often (usually every pay period) that big door is opened and your contributions go in. Inside that garage are various investments for you to choose from. You actually have to go inside the garage, look around at the options, and choose which ones you want your contributions to go into."

"Some investments are potentially very risky but, at the same time, have the potential for large rewards. On the other hand, some investments provide little to no risk and, as a result, provide little to no return. How well you pick your investments will have a big impact on the value of your 401(k) in retirement and, hence, your standard of living at that time. Will you have enough saved to buy that house you've always wanted or to visit the exotic places in the world that you dreamed of traveling to? It all depends, in large part, on the investment choices you make within your 401(k)."

"Over the last few decades, your contributions were being deposited into the most conservative of investments, which essentially acted as a savings account. This means that your 401(k) contributions were going into an investment that did not intend to grow your money. Rather, the main goal was to preserve your money (essentially keep the balance the same) and earn modest interest every month. As a result, you missed out on decades' worth of substantially more growth."

Suffice it to say, she was flabbergasted that she had not known the basics of her 401(k). She, like most clients I have worked with, just assumed the 401(k) would somehow grow her money over time. What ultimately had happened is her 401(k) contributions went into a money market mutual fund, and they stayed in that fund for decades. She was not invested in any other asset class (e.g., bonds and stocks) and because of this, she lost out on having a substantially larger retirement fund and a more bountiful retirement—the difference between having $1,000 per month and $4,000 per month. Unfortunately for her, it was too late. Let's make sure this doesn't happen to you. Let's get started on the basics!

Brief History of the 401(k)

The Revenue Act of 1978 included a provision that became Internal Revenue Code (IRC) Sec. 401(k). To spare you yet another discussion surrounding rules, laws, and regulations, let's just agree that this is when and how the 401(k) was created. Since its inception, the 401(k) has been another main source of retirement savings for a majority of Americans. In fact, for many Americans, particularly from younger generations who will never have a company pension, the 401(k) has become the third source of retirement income, coupled with personal savings (including IRAs) and social security.

Remember from our prior discussion that, before the 401(k), one of the main benefits companies offered was a pension. For employees, this was great because the responsibility of setting aside money (saving) and then subsequent investment of that money, as well as all the administrative tasks (e.g., keeping track of balances, making deposits, cutting and mailing pension checks), was that of the employer. With the 401(k), some of the most major responsibilities now rest with you and me, the employees.

Just like with IRAs, I want you to think of a 401(k) as a big, empty garage building with barbed wire fencing surrounding it. At its essence, this is all a 401(k) represents: an account created by your employer on your behalf. You have the ability to refuse participation in the 401(k), but keep in mind, 401(k)s are becoming one of the main sources of our retirement income, replacing pensions. So, it might be a good idea to at least consider it.

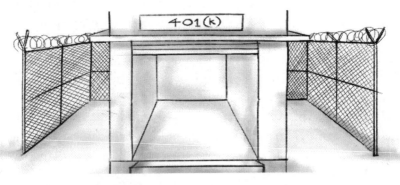

Let's assume you decide to participate in your company's 401(k) plan. What happens next? Well, usually, first, you must determine how much of your paycheck you want your employer to contribute to your 401(k). For example, let's imagine that your paycheck is for $1,000, and you decide you can afford to invest 5% of this amount each pay period. Thus, $50 per pay period would be deposited into your 401(k).

As an incentive to get employees to actually participate in their 401(k)s, many employers will offer a company 401(k) match. That is, your employer will contribute a certain amount of money (out of their own pocket and represented in red in the above illustration) to your 401(k) based on your contribution amount. For example, let's say that your employer will match your contribution 50%, dollar-for-dollar, on the first 5%.[26] This means your employer would add an additional deposit of $25 for every $50 you contributed to your 401 (k). So even though you only contributed $50, your account balance will read $75. This is what is commonly referred to as "free money." It's really not much more difficult than this.

So, now you have a pile of cash in your 401(k). Over time, as you contribute more and more to your 401(k), that pile of cash should grow in size; this is in essence how the 401(k) helps you save for retirement. However, we are not done yet. Once you have a pile of cash in your 401(k), what will you do? After all, the responsibility is now on you to make investment choices within the 401(k), and whether your investment choices are wise will determine your account performance and, ultimately, how much money you will have saved for retirement. Does this seem daunting? Fear not!

I devoted the first few chapters of this book to educating you on exactly how to make these investment choices. Do you remember the buckets? Don't forget the basics; keep it simple. Just like with IRAs, there will be three buckets of investing within your 401(k): cash, bonds, and stocks.

---

26   Matching contributions, if offered by an employer, can vary greatly. The figures presented here are purely hypothetical, and you will want to check with your benefits department for details surrounding your particular plan.

It really is that simple! Even still, I understand that this may seem daunting, especially since it is now up to you to actually go into your 401(k) and make investment decisions. Although more and more companies seem to be offering their employees free financial advice regarding investments within their 401(k), the responsibility ultimately rests on our (i.e., employees) shoulders. Fret not! The first few chapters of this book are devoted to educating you on exactly how to do this. You can always go back and reread those chapters to refresh your knowledge.

Investments within a 401(k)

Since a 401(k) is an employer-sponsored retirement account, it is your employer's responsibility to open and manage the logistics of the 401(k). Part of this responsibility includes choosing what types of investments will be available for you to invest in within your 401(k).

Essentially, your employer will open a 401(k) with a financial firm (usually called an *administrator*) that then creates a "garage" for you and encloses that garage in barbed wire (more on this momentarily). That financial firm and your employer work together to determine what sorts of investments they will make available to you within your 401(k). Will you be able to trade individual stocks or bonds? Will you be able to purchase mutual funds?

Typically, the majority of 401(k)s will restrict their employees to investing in mutual funds and only a handful at that. The mutual funds within most 401(k)s will usually represent the three asset classes: cash, bonds, and stocks. In other words, there will probably be one or two money market mutual fund cash investments, a few stock mutual funds representing value, growth, and blended, as well as large-, medium- and small-capitalizations, and then bond mutual funds representing short-, intermediate-, and long-term maturities of government, corporate, and blended bonds. As we mentioned in Chapter 7 discussing asset allocation, you will be able to choose your own asset allocation and then adjust accordingly as time progresses. In addition, it is becoming even more popular for 401(k)s to offer asset allocation funds and age based funds.

Limiting 401(k)s to mutual funds might be a good idea. After all, as we learned in Chapter 6, a mutual fund will provide you with many benefits, such as professional management of your money and diversification. Can you imagine the potential horror stories if individuals were allowed to "play" in the stock market with their 401(k) retirement savings?

TAXATION

Another important feature of the 401(k) is taxation. If you will please recall that in Chapter 8, we discussed capital gain and dividend taxation. Taxation of capital gains and dividends will usually diminish the amount of your investment (by the amount of taxes paid on any gains and/or dividends). A unique feature of a 401(k) account is that while your money is in a 401(k), no capital gain nor dividend taxation occurs, just as with a Traditional IRA and Roth IRA.

You could invest $10,000 into a stock and sell it for $1 million (a $990,000 capital gain), and you would not owe capital gains taxes on the earnings while in the 401(k), so you could reinvest the whole $990,000. Compare this to a regular investment account, which could see taxes on the $990,000 as high as 39%. After the 39% capital gains taxation, you would have around $604,000 to reinvest. Thus, by not having to pay capital gain or dividend taxes, you are keeping more of your money and are able to then reinvest those proceeds to hopefully continue to grow your account for retirement. Avoidance of capital gain and dividend taxation is a feature unique to accounts such as a 401(k).[27]

At this point, I would like to discuss the qualities and differences between two of the most common 401(k) plans: pre-tax (traditional) and after-tax (Roth) 401(k)s.

Traditional 401(k)s

Prior to 2006, 401(k)s were established under what is commonly referred to as a traditional plan. To understand traditional plans, we must once again briefly discuss the ever-fun topic of taxes. So please keep up the good work and bear with me a bit longer.

Contributions to a Traditional 401(k) are deducted from your paycheck pre-tax. For example, let's assume your gross paycheck is for $1,500 (gross meaning before taxes or deductions). Let's also assume you have elected a 5% traditional 401(k) deduction. This means that $75 will be withdrawn from the $1,500 gross paycheck and deposited into your 401(k), reducing your paycheck to $1,425, which is the amount of income reported to the IRS (i.e., the amount income taxes will be assessed on). Essentially, the $75 401(k) contribution has flown under the radar of income taxation. This has two potential benefits. First, your taxable income on the whole could be substantially lowered because, instead of reporting $1,500 to the IRS, you are now reporting the lower amount of $1,425. This could help you report a lower income for the year and owe less taxes. Second, your $75 tax-free (or I should say "tax-delayed") contribution, while invested, may not owe capital gains taxes. As stated earlier, this means that while you are investing your money inside the 401(k), you will not owe capital gains or dividend taxes.[28] This should help you keep more of your money and, subsequently, grow your retirement savings more quickly.

Now, here is the kicker. We have just discussed that, with Traditional 401(k)s, your contributions are pre-tax (e.g., the $75 contribution). Do you think the IRS has a compassionate heart and will allow us to avoid

---

27 Tax laws can change, so please consult with a tax advisor prior to any investment decision.

28 Please refer to Chapter 8 for a discussion surrounding taxes and investing.

income tax on this money? If you believe so, I sincerely congratulate you on your optimism. Unfortunately, the IRS will eventually require you to pay tax on that money. So, when does that happen?

When you contribute money to a traditional 401(k), that money is pre-tax (as we have just discussed), and once in the 401(k), your investment earnings will not be taxed (e.g., capital gains, dividends). However, when you withdraw money from a Traditional 401(k), income taxes will be assessed, not when you withdraw the money, but rather, when you file your tax return for the year. You will be required to calculate and report the taxes owed. So, why would delaying income taxation potentially benefit you? After all, you're still paying, just at a later date.

Just like with IRAs, the same concepts hold true for 401(k)s. For example, let's assume you are in a career that pays quite well, and as a result, you are in a high tax bracket (e.g., 39%). However, you expect that when you retire, you will not be working, or if you will be working, it would be part-time. As a result, you expect to be in a much lower income tax bracket in retirement (e.g., 15%). Would you rather pay 39% in income taxes now or 15% in income taxes later?

ROTH 401(k)

The Roth 401(k) became available to U.S. employees (assuming their companies offered it) in 2006. So, what is a Roth 401(k), and how does it compare to a Traditional 401(k)?

A Roth 401(k) has similar features as a Traditional 401(k) with the exception of when and how income taxation is applied. A Roth 401(k) is still a big garage building with barbed wire around it and investments inside it. Once inside the Roth 401(k), investment taxation is avoided (e.g., capital gains and dividend taxation).

One of the key differences between a Roth 401(k) and Traditional 401(k) is how contributions are taxed. Contributions to your Roth 401(k) are after-tax contributions. Let's assume your gross paycheck is for $1,500, and after all applicable taxes (e.g., FICA, SSI), your net paycheck is $1,250 and you have elected to have a 5% Roth 401(k) contribution. This means your 5% is calculated based on the net paycheck amount of $1,250 for a total Roth 401(k) contribution of $62.50. In essence, since this contribution is coming out of your net paycheck (i.e., income taxes already levied), you will not owe income tax on the $62.50, even upon withdrawal in later years. So, if you are perhaps in a low tax bracket during your earning years (e.g., 15%), but anticipate being in a higher tax bracket in retirement (e.g., 39%), a Roth 401(k) may make sense. After all, would you rather pay 15% in taxes now or 39% in taxes later?

Vesting

Jane Doe 401 (k) Statement

Date: January 1, 2010 – December 31, 2010

Total Account Balance: $40,000
Vested Account Balance: $32,000

Employee: $32,000

Employer: $8,000

In the previous pages, we discussed how an employer may offer a company 401(k) match as an incentive for the employee to save for retirement. An employer may deposit company monies into the employee's 401(k) account. This means that many 401(k)s will have co-mingled contributions—that of the employee and that of the employer—all within the employee's 401(k). Often, 401(k) statements will show the entire account balance of the 401(k), let's say $40,000, but then divide that balance between the employee contribution and the employer contribution.

The amounts you have contributed (i.e., employee contributions), you are entitled to immediately (i.e., these amounts are vested). But what about the employer contributions? Are you entitled to those? This is where vesting can get tricky because the answer to this question depends on what your company has decided to do. Some employers will immediately vest employer contributions. Once employer contributions are deposited into your account, they become your monies immediately. Other employers may have vesting schedules. For example, they may allow you to vest in 25% of employer contributions after one year of service, 50% after three years of service, and so on.

So, the next time you view your 401(k) account balance, you will want to pay particular attention to your vested account balance, which could be a combination of both employee (you) and employer contributions. Whatever the case, the vested balance is what you are entitled to.

Withdrawals

The next feature of a 401(k) is withdrawals. From my professional experience, most clients assumed that, since the money in their 401(k) was theirs (vested), they could then withdraw that money whenever they wanted. That is not the case.

Since the 401(k) was established through an Internal Revenue Code, the Internal Revenue Service (IRS) establishes the rules for 401(k)s. The rules surrounding when you can withdraw money from your 401(k) can be quite complicated. To keep it simple, while you are an active employee, you generally are not able to withdraw monies from your 401(k) unless you have what the IRS classifies as a hardship, and even then, it can be a tedious undertaking and may be dependent on whether your employer has followed the necessary regulations to allow such a withdrawal. A hardship might include some of the following: funeral expenses, principal residence purchase, or tuition payment and educational expenses.[29]

Many life events occur that a lot of us might consider hardships (for example, being laid off and needing money to pay a mortgage or purchase food) but that, in the eyes of the IRS, are not hardships and would negate your ability to withdraw funds. It may sound unfair since it is your money, but these are the rules we must play by and they are set by the IRS. This is why, in our 401(k) illustration, a barbed wire fence surrounds the 401(k). The imagery of the barbed wire reflects

---

29 Please consult your 401(k) plan and/or a competent tax advisor prior to making any investment decisions. The material provided here is for informational purposes and may not reflect current tax law.

the difficulty of removing funds from a 401(k). Conversely, with IRAs, there is no barbed wire fence indicating the typical ease with which withdrawals from IRAs can occur.

Termination of Employment

Generally, while we are employed and have a 401(k), accessing the monies within the 401(k) is rather difficult if not seemingly impossible. However, once we leave our employer, whether voluntarily (e.g., job change, retirement) or involuntary (e.g., layoff), we usually have more flexibility to access our funds.

Keep 401(k) with Company

Often, if your 401(k) balance is above a certain amount (usually around $5,000), then your company may allow you to keep your balance within the 401(k), even though you no longer work for the company. There are potential pros and cons associated with leaving your balance in your company 401(k).

One of the pros is that you get to keep your asset allocation—the investments you have been contributing to perhaps for decades. Maybe you are fond of the investments within the 401(k) and want to stay invested in them. Also, you might be familiar with the "mechanics" of your 401(k), such as the website and/or the customer service aspects.

However, accessing monies from the 401(k), even after separation of employment, can be tedious at best. You usually have to complete and submit paperwork, wait for confirmation of liquidation of investment to generate the cash you need, and then wait for a check to be mailed to you (because most 401(k)s do not have electronic funds transfer services). Additionally, by keeping the funds with your previous employer, you are missing out on potentially hundreds of other investment options offered through many IRAs. As opposed to having only a dozen or so mutual funds, you could potentially have access to thousands of mutual funds in addition to individual stocks, bonds, and ETFs.

Cash Out

Extremely inadvisable, a cash out might be an option upon separation of employment. Simply, when you cash out, you are requesting the investments within your 401(k) be liquidated (i.e., sold) and the proceeds sent to you. It might be nice to have the cash sent electronically to your bank, but 401(k) distributions are usually in the form of a check that will be mailed to you.

Regardless of the method of receiving your cash, cashing out of a 401(k) will carry with it tremendous tax consequences. For starters, upon a cash out, your 401(k) will be required to withhold 20% of your total balance for income tax (per IRS rules). This means that right off the top you will "lose" 20%. If your account balance is $40,000, your check will be for $32,000. Also, when you file your tax return, you may owe more in income tax, and if you are under age 59.5 and initiate a cash out, you will potentially owe a 10% penalty tax.

Without getting into the nitty-gritty, cash outs are usually inadvisable. Even if you need cash from the 401(k), there are options that will allow you this access while minimizing taxation, such as rolling over your 401(k) balance to an IRA.

Rollovers

Understanding the basics of 401(k) rollovers is imperative. If a rollover is not done properly, there could be massive tax consequences, not to mention a potential delay in your retirement.

Rollovers are generally initiated when you are no longer working for the employer through whom you have your 401(k). Perhaps you are separated from employment through retirement, termination, or a change in employer. Whatever the case, the moment you are no longer working for an employer is the moment you usually need to decide whether to rollover your 401(k). There are generally two rollover methods: *Direct Rollover* and *Indirect Rollover*.

Direct Rollover

A direct rollover is a transfer of assets from a 401(k) to a similar, or like, IRA, referred to as a "like-to-like" transfer. This means that if you have a Traditional 401(k), you will need to transfer those assets to a Traditional IRA. If you have a Roth 401(k), you will need to transfer those assets to a Roth IRA.

Once you have a like IRA opened, you will then instruct your 401(k) that you would like to initiate a direct rollover to an IRA. There are a few important steps that must now happen. First, your 401(k) administrator will liquidate (i.e., sell) any investments you might have within the 401(k), which will mean you will end up with a pile of cash within your 401(k). Depending upon the investments, this liquidation process can take a few days.

Upon settlement of the liquidation (and subsequent pile of cash), your 401(k) administrator will cut a physical check. Your 401(k) administrator *should* know the appropriate steps, but it will bode you well to know what needs to happen.

Most importantly, the check should be made payable to the IRA custodian for your benefit. For example, let's assume you opened an IRA, in your name, with ABC Brokerage. The 401(k) direct rollover check should read:

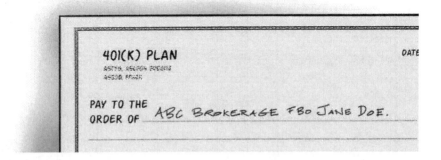

This is *imperative* because, in the eyes of the IRS, the money in your 401(k) has not been made payable to you. It has been made payable to your new IRA custodian for your benefit. As a result, it's as if the money never left a tax sheltered account.

Sometimes, the check will be mailed directly to you, at which point you do *nothing* more than mail it to your new IRA custodian. You *do not* endorse the check or do anything other than send it off to your new IRA. Other times, the direct rollover check will be mailed directly to the new IRA custodian in which case you simply wait for the money to be deposited into your new IRA. This brings up an important point.

While in the 401(k), you might have obtained an asset allocation. For example, a mixture of cash, bond, and stock mutual funds. As we just learned though, once you initiate a direct rollover, all those assets are liquidated and you are left with cash. Once this cash is deposited into your new IRA, you will need to go into your IRA and once again determine an asset allocation and invest your money.

To some of us, this may sound disheartening for any number of reasons. Perhaps you were fond of the investments within your 401(k). Perhaps you do not want to, once again, have to engage in determining a new asset allocation and deciding on new investments. I get it, but the good news is that most IRAs will allow you broader access to a wide range of investments.

The investments provided to you within your 401(k) were determined by your employer and the 401(k) administrator. For the most part, 401(k)s offer only a handful of mutual funds: a few cash mutual funds, a couple of bond mutual funds, and a few stock mutual funds (also perhaps a few asset allocation and target date mutual funds). IRAs, on the other hand, usually allow you access to hundreds if not thousands of mutual funds. Moreover, most IRAs will also allow you to trade individual bonds, stocks, and even ETFs.

Indirect Rollover

Although typically not advisable, an indirect rollover is another available option upon separation of employment. An indirect rollover is very similar to a direct rollover in so much as you are liquidating your investments within your 401(k) and receiving a check. However, with indirect rollovers, checks will be made payable directly to you—in your name. This is vastly different than a check being made payable to your new IRA for your benefit (fbo) and can have massive tax consequences.

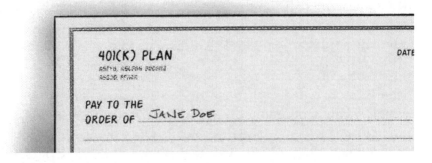

Since the check is made payable to you, in the eyes of the IRS, you have taken a distribution from your 401(k), which means the IRS will now levy income taxation on the amount you take out. If you are under age 59.5, you may be subject to an additional 10% early withdrawal penalty. Both of these taxes (income and the potential penalty tax) will be mitigated when you file your tax return. However, there is a third "tax" that you will experience.

Since with an indirect rollover you are taking possession of the money, your 401(k) administrator is required by IRS law to withhold 20% of your distribution amount as a sort of *pre-payment* of taxes due. For example, if your 401(k) balance is $100,000 and you initiate an indirect rollover, your check amount will be for $80,000. That's right! Your 401(k) administrator will legally have to withhold 20% or $20,000 as an estimated income tax payment and send this amount to the IRS.

There is a way you can avoid this potential for income taxation and early penalty taxation: deposit the full $100,000 into an IRA within 60 days. If your indirect rollover check is for $80,000, and you deposit that into a like IRA within 60 days, you still need to come up with the "missing" $20,000. If you are able to come up with the $20,000, then you can have the withheld amount refunded during tax time. If you do not, then during tax time, the IRS will assume you withdrew the $20,000 and that amount will be subject to income taxation and perhaps early withdrawal penalties.

The IRS rules surrounding 401(k) and IRA taxation can be complex, are ever-changing, and are extremely important to understand. Given the complexities, please know that an indirect rollover is usually not advisable. The potential taxes and penalties, not to mention the mandatory 20% withholding, can be quite large. If you are hard-pressed for money, you can simply initiate a *direct rollover* to a like IRA, which would be tax and penalty free, and then once the money is deposited into the IRA, you can quite easily withdraw money whenever you want. Opening an IRA, contacting the 401(k) administrator, waiting for liquidation of your 401(k) investments, waiting for the check to arrive, sending the check to your new IRA custodian, waiting on them to deposit the check into your IRA, and then requesting money be sent to your bank can take quite some time, but you will ultimately benefit in the long run over initiating an indirect rollover.

Until now, we have focused on 401(k) plans. It should be noted that 401(k) retirement plans are usually only offered by private companies—private in the sense that they are non-government or non-profit companies (think of Apple® or Wal-Mart®). What about those of us who do not work for private companies and instead work for government entities or non-profit groups, including teachers, government workers, and the like?

403(b) and 457 Retirement Plans

Practical experience suggests that government entities generally "play" under different rules than the rest of us. I am not being critical of this, but it seems to be a fact. For example, 457 plans generally do not assess a 10% penalty for withdrawing money prior to age 59.5. Also, 457 plans may allow more lenient hardship withdrawal reasons for accessing 457 retirement money while still employed. With that said, if you participate in one of these plans, it would behoove you to talk with your benefits representative to learn about the specifics surrounding withdrawals and investment options.

The overriding point I want to stress is that these plans (457 and 403(b)) share many of the same basic characteristics with 401(k)s. That is, 457s and 403(b)s are simply big, empty accounts (*garage buildings*) that you deposit money into from payroll/paycheck deductions, and once your money is deposited into these accounts, you will need to invest it amongst the three main asset classes. Other than that, they may have different names and a few unique characteristics (e.g., more lenient withdrawal options, different investment choices). Simple enough, right?

SEP & SIMPLE IRAs

Finally, we will spend a brief time covering SIMPLE & SEP IRAs. You might be asking yourself why we are having a discussion on IRAs in a chapter devoted to 401(k)s as opposed to in our prior chapter on IRAs. SEP & SIMPLE IRAs are essentially the 401(k) *equivalents* for small businesses. Let's explain this a bit further.

First, SIMPLE stands for *Savings Incentive Match Plan for Employees* and SEP stands for *Simplified Employee Pension*. These are the 401(k) equivalents for small businesses. Establishing and maintaining a 401(k) plan is often a very costly undertaking and only feasible for larger corporations (think of a large national bank or large retailer). But what about small companies that might have a few dozen or so employees? That is where the SEP and SIMPLE IRAs come into play.

Now, even though IRA is in the name, these plans act more as company-sponsored retirement plans, just like the 401(k) we previously discussed. However, there are many nuisances as to what type of small business can open a SEP or SIMPLE, such as the number of the business's employees, whether another employer plan is being offered, and mandatory employer contributions. These are just a few of the many legal nuances these types of plans have. For the sake of this introductory book, we will forego a deep dive into these various elements. For now, we'll stick to the basics.

Generally, a SIMPLE IRA is for businesses that employ less than 100 employees, whereas a SEP IRA is for businesses that employ one or more employees. Does that sound confusing? Essentially, for a small business that employs just a handful of personnel, the SEP IRA might be something to consider. For the larger small businesses, which perhaps employ dozens of employees, yet less than one hundred, a SIMPLE IRA might be an appropriate plan.

If you are a small business owner, hopefully this introduction into the two most common small business retirement plans will provide you with some "ammo" to go out and engage in further research. Until then, the overriding point is that these plans act similarly to the tax-sheltered accounts we have already been discussing (e.g., 401(k)s and IRAs). That is, with these two types of plans, an employee will indicate how much of their pay to contribute into the account. The employer may decide to contribute money into the employee's account as well (i.e., a matching contribution). Regardless, once in the account, the employee will then need to invest his or her money, and once again, how does he or she do this?

He or she will use the three buckets of investing: cash, bonds and stocks. The employee will want to obtain an asset allocation so that his or her retirement money within these accounts has the potential to grow over time—for retirement. So, SEP and SIMPLE IRAs are tax-sheltered retirement accounts for small businesses and act similarly to 401(k) and IRA accounts.

Summary

The retirement dreams of many Americans will be dependent upon how well they have saved for retirement during their working years. With the eventual departure of the employer pension plan, one of the main retirement accounts will be the 401(k).

> Note: You will most likely hear pensions referred to as *Defined Benefit Plans* and employer sponsored plans (e.g., 401(k), 457) referred to as *Defined Contribution Plans*.

At its core, a 401(k) is very similar to an IRA in so much as a 401(k) is simply an account in which you deposit money. Often, your employer will also contribute money, called a matching contribution. Once money is in your 401(k), you will need to go inside the 401(k) and make investment decisions, or allocate you assets. Since your employer established and maintains the 401(k) on your behalf, they have a say as to what types of investments are offered in the 401(k), and you are limited to what they offer. Usually, 401(k)s will only offer mutual funds, but these mutual funds will most likely cover the three main asset classes.

There will be a few cash mutual funds (e.g., money market mutual funds or stable value funds), a few bond mutual funds, a few stock mutual funds, and even asset allocation and target date funds.

It is imperative that you familiarize yourself with what investments are offered in your 401(k) and that you then make an appropriate asset allocation. You do not want to end up only investing in cash investments and then, many years or decades later, realize you missed out on potential growth.

One of the main takeaways are the concepts surrounding rollovers from 401(k)s. Many people run into problems with these types of transactions, usually with dramatic tax consequences. When you separate from employment, you may decide to leave your 401(k) with your employer, initiate a direct rollover or an indirect rollover, or cash out of your 401(k).

As previously discussed, a cash out is probably the most inadvisable form of distribution from a 401(k). Sure, with a cash out you are able to get your hands on your money, but there may be massive tax consequences such as income tax (including a 20% estimated income tax withholding) and early withdrawal penalties for those of us under age 59.5.

An *Indirect Rollover* is another distribution option from a 401(k), but will also carry with it the potential for massive tax consequences. First of all, when initiating an indirect rollover, your 401(k) will send you a rollover check made payable directly to you. This means, in the eyes of the IRS, that you have taken possession of the money that was in your 401(k) and as a result, taxes must be assessed. Your 401(k) is mandated by law to withhold 20% of the distribution as estimated income taxation and if you do not deposit the 20% withholding amount into an IRA within 60 days, then that amount may be viewed as a distribution by the IRS. When you file your tax return for the year, that amount could be subject to income taxation and an early withdrawal penalty (if you are under age 59.5).

One of the most common, and probably most appropriate, distribution options is to initiate a *direct rollover* to a like IRA. Yes, this means you will have to liquidate the investments within your 401(k) and essentially "start over" in the IRA, but there are potentially many benefits in doing this. Most 401(k)s provide only a handful of mutual funds. On the other hand, IRAs generally allow access to a plethora of investments, including hundreds if not thousands of different mutual funds, individual stocks, bonds, and ETFs.

Withdrawing money from a 401(k) can be a rather tedious proposition with the potential for massive tax consequences. However, once your 401(k) money is deposited into a like IRA, withdrawing money becomes a lot easier. Withdrawing money from an IRA can be a rather simple undertaking with the potential to have money deposited into a bank account within days. Although this is generally not advisable pre-retirement, the withdrawal features of IRAs can be a benefit should you run into an emergency.

Chapter 12

Brokerage Accounts

At this point in our discussion, we have digested quite a bit of information surrounding a variety of topics related to investing (asset classes, asset allocation, taxation, 401(k)s, etc.). It is my sincere hope that you are now starting to understand the basics of investing (even if just a little bit), and if you are, I congratulate you! But let me pose another question: how can you actually participate in the various investments we have been discussing? Do you need to open an account somewhere, and if so, where is that somewhere? Will you need to have a minimum amount of money to invest to open one of these accounts? Where will you start? Once again, in an attempt to keep it simple, I will address two types of companies you will work with in order to engage in investing: banks and brokerage firms.

Banks

I imagine a majority of us reading this book have interacted with a bank at some point in our lives and that we are quite familiar with how banks operate. As such, our discussion of banks will be quite fleeting.

Banks are generally in the business of providing deposit accounts (e.g., savings and checking accounts), as well as in the lending business (e.g., home, auto, and car loans). If a bank offers investments, they are usually of the mundane variety and within the cash bucket (i.e., savings, checking, certificates of deposit, and money market accounts). For example, your local bank may offer an Individual Retirement

Account (IRA), but as we learned in Chapter 10, all an IRA consists of is a blank building and inside that building are various investments to chose from. An IRA at a bank will usually only consist of cash investments, such as money market accounts or certificates of deposit. Other investments, such as stocks and bonds, are usually not offered at banks. So, if you want exposure to the stock and/or bond markets, you will need to consider opening an account with a brokerage firm. Your local bank may offer brokerage accounts separate from its banking services.

Brokerage Firms

Unlike banks, brokerage firms are in the business of facilitating trading within the stock and bond markets, as well as providing financial advice and education. There are two main types of brokerage firms: *Discount Brokerage Firms* and *Full-Service Brokerage Firms*. Before we delve into a discussion surrounding the two types of brokerage firms, let's first touch on some basic investment market ideas.

History suggests that the New York Stock Exchange (NYSE), perhaps the powerhouse of stock market exchanges, initially began under a buttonwood tree in New York. That's right, individuals would gather under a tree and engage in stock trading. Fast forward a few hundred years, and the stock markets in the US have become sophisticated, elaborate, and pivotal aspects of the U.S. capitalist economy.

Essentially, the stock market is where stock buyers and sellers meet to engage in trading. For exchanges, such as the NYSE, buyers and sellers meet face-to-face in a physical location (i.e., Wall Street). There are also electronic exchanges, such as the NASDAQ, in which all trading is completed electronically through the internet, and no face-to-face interaction occurs. In either case, how do you, the investor, obtain access to these markets?

It is not probable that you would venture down Wall Street, knock on the door of the NYSE, and ask to trade stock or sign into the electronic trading system of the NASDAQ and engage in investing. So, what do you do?

Essentially, you have the stock market on one end and you on the other. In order to access these markets, you are generally going to need a middle man, and that is what we refer to as a broker. Let me present to you with a brief illustration that visually encapsulates this concept:

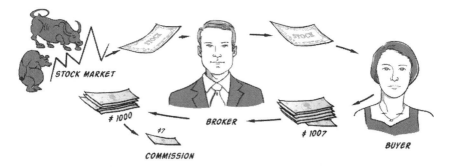

The above illustration depicts a very basic, yet typical, brokerage transaction. We have the stock market to the far left and you, the investor (or the buyer), to the far right. The broker is your middleman, who will take trading instructions from you and then go into the stock market and act on your behalf. The broker is providing you a service. In fact, brokers usually provide you many services, such as producing tax documents, tracking the *cost basis* of your stock trades, providing statements, and online accounts. As a result, the broker will most likely charge you a fee for his/her work. One of the most common fees you will be presented with is a *commission*.

Commission

In the above illustration, our investor wants to purchase $1,000 of a particular stock. However, her broker charges a $7 commission for each trade. As a result, our investor will need to deposit $1,007 with her broker at which point the broker will "pocket" the $7 and then purchase $1,000 worth of stocks in the stock market. Once purchased, the broker will deposit the stock into the investor's account. If our investor decides to subsequently sell the stock, the process repeats itself, including another commission charge. For example, if our investor's initial purchase of $1,000 was sold for $1,500 she would receive $1,493 because $7 was withheld as a commission. Also, commissions are usually charged regardless of the amount of money you are investing.

For example, if you wanted to buy one share of a stock trading at $10 per share, you would need to provide your broker with $17.

In reality, commissions on investing trades can vary enormously and are largely dependent upon what type of brokerage firm you choose to invest with (more on this in a bit). In fact, prior to the advent of discount brokerage firms, which really took off with the dawn of the internet, commissions varied greatly and could even see charges as high as thousands of dollars.

As a result, it was usually quite expensive to place trades. For example, if you wanted to invest $1,000 and the commission was $245, you would need to deposit $1,245 after which you would be left with a $1,000 investment. This is almost a 25% charge (or put another way, a 25% loss) right off the bat. The same would usually happen when you sold your investment. For example, let's assume your $1,000 investment grew to $1,500, and you sold it. After a $245 commission, you would be left with $1,255. As you can see, these commissions could certainly add up, and this is one of the main reasons why, in the past, access to the securities markets (i.e., investing) was limited to the wealthy. This has all changed with the advent of the *discount brokerage firm*.

Discount Brokerage Firms

Discount brokerage firms tailor their services to the "do it yourself" investor. These types of investors usually know what they want to do and when they want to do it, and they do not want nor need the assistance of financial professionals (e.g., financial advisors).

Discount brokerage firms are commonly online based. You will open your account online, fund your account online, and place trades online. For the most part, everything will be online. Usually, these firms will have a support staff that you can reach by telephone and who can assist you with a host of items, such as navigating the website, and can even walk you through how to place trades. These firms may have a few physical locations (i.e., branches) spread throughout the country, but they will most likely be made up of skeleton crews who are there to answer and assist with basic matters. Additionally, since these accounts are tailored to the do-it-yourself investor, you will generally have no access to someone that will provide you with advice or guidance on how to invest your money. However, many of these firms will provide you with an absolute plethora of online resources from educational articles and videos to financial calculators.

Because you are essentially doing everything yourself, these brokerage firms will be able to charge you minimal commissions. Full-service brokerage firms, on the other hand, provide all sorts of specialized services and advice and, as a result, can charge hundreds of dollars in commissions. According to the *Barron's Online Broker Survey 2014*, the average stock commission rate was $6.52 per trade (rating of 20 different discount brokerage firms).

Another distinguishing feature of discount brokerage accounts is their low initial opening deposit amounts ranging from just a few hundred dollars to thousands of dollars. In fact, some discount firms may have no minimum deposit amount required at all. I realize that "low" is relative to the individual investor. Some of you may not have a few hundred dollars to initially deposit into a brokerage account, and I empathize with that, but here is a hint. Often, you can open a brokerage account, link up your bank account, transfer in the minimum amount required, and then subsequently transfer that amount back to your bank account. In this instance, you will have an open brokerage account with no money in it. When you are ready to place a trade, you can then transfer money (in whatever amount) to your brokerage account. There are a few things you need to consider though.

First, some discount brokerage firms may not only require an initial deposit, but also require you maintain an ongoing minimum balance. For example, they may require you deposit $2,000 to open an account and then maintain at least a $500 balance; otherwise, you may receive a "naughty" letter in the mail reminding you to increase the balance or close the account. Secondly, when transferring funds electronically from a bank account to a brokerage account (or vice versa), there can be a delay in how quickly your money will be available to you. From my experience, these electronic fund transfers can take a few days to complete. Also, when you sell a stock, the money from that stock sale usually is not available to you for three business days, which adds time onto the electronic fund transfer timing. Nevertheless, discount brokerage firms are a viable option even for novice investors and those investors without much money to invest.

Our discussion has focused on items I believe you will run into should you decide to open an account with a discount brokerage firm. Please keep in mind that each firm will have its own balance requirements (if any), commission schedule, and online features. I have provided you with some useful information below.[30]

Table 12.1 Discount Brokerage Fees & Balance Requirements

Firm	Cost Per Stock Trade	Minimum Balance
Charles Schwab®	$8.95	$1,000
Scottrade®	$7.00	$2,500
TD Ameritrade®	$9.99	$0
E*TRADE®	$9.99	NA

Table 12.1 shows some of the more well-known discount brokerage firms along with pertinent information pertaining to commissions on (cost per) stock trades and minimum balance requirements (if any). If you consider opening an account with one of these firms, I would first suggest perusing each firm's website and see which one stands out to you. As you can see in the table, the cost per stock trade is relatively low at each firm with only a few dollars separating them. However, the services they provide might be more important for you. For example, will you want 24-hour customer service that you can call? Will you want a lot of online educational resources? Perhaps, you only really want an aesthetically pleasing site? Whatever the case, researching first can be beneficial, and I highly recommend that you visit each site.

30 Data obtained directly from the source website(s) and is subject to change. Please consult the respective company website for the most recent data.

Full-Service Brokerage Firms

If discount brokerage firms are for the do-it-yourself investor, full-service brokerage firms are for those investors seeking a hands off approach to investing. These investors are willing to pay more in fees and commissions to have professional management of their investments, including all the bells and whistles that come with it.

One important aspect of full-service brokerage firms is that you do not work directly with the firm as you would with a discount broker. Instead, you need to have a relationship with one of the firm's representatives, often referred to as Financial Advisors. There are numerous ways for you to develop a relationship with one of the firm's financial advisors. Perhaps you have had a financial advisor send you a letter through the mail soliciting his/her services. Other financial advisors may hold seminars in which they introduce themselves to you. Alternatively, you could call the firm and inquire about a financial advisor in your area. In fact, some firms may allow you to enter your inquiry electronically through their websites and the firm will then pair you up with an advisor near you. Whatever the case, you need to have a relationship with a financial advisor in order to have an account with a full-service brokerage firm.

Remember from our prior discussion that discount brokerage firms simply provide you with an outlet to the financial markets. You will make your own investment choices, place your own trades, and manage your own money. Discount brokerage firms usually provide you with a wealth of financial education, but actually investing and managing your money are all left up to you. When you work with a financial advisor, all the work rests on the shoulders of your financial advisor. But you won't be left out of the picture entirely. Quite the contrary, your financial advisor should be in regular communication with you so that you know what he/she is doing and when and why he/she is doing it. It is my hope that this book will give you at least a basic understanding of what your advisor is doing and why.

As we will see, the services provided by a financial advisor can be quite extensive. However, the most basic (and perhaps most important) service delivered by a financial advisor is to provide you with asset allocation and diversification. In other words, the financial advisor will determine how much of your money goes into each bucket (i.e., asset allocation) and then subsequently diversify your monies within each bucket (i.e., diversification). After reading the first few chapters of this book, as well as the chapter on asset allocation and diversification, you should have at least a basic understanding of how to do this yourself. However, a financial advisor typically specializes in asset allocation and diversification by continually watching the financial markets and keeping abreast of economic conditions. Based on this analysis, your financial advisor may recommend that you alter your diversification. For example, your advisor may determine that the economy will enter a contractionary period and, as a result, recommend that you decrease your growth stocks (i.e., electronics) and increase your value stock (i.e., toilet paper). If instead your advisor determines that economic conditions may warrant an increase in interest rates, he/she may suggest you limit your bond exposure since when interest rates increase, bond prices decrease.

In essence, these types of analyses and ongoing services are the "bread and butter" of what financial advisors are supposed to do for you. Additionally, many financial advisors go above and beyond by offering all sorts of ancillary services. These services can include the following: tax planning and preparation, college planning, budgeting recommendations, retirement planning, and social security income planning. Now, because you are receiving all these services, you should expect the fees and commissions you pay to be substantially higher than discount brokerage accounts.

First, financial advisors can earn compensation in many ways. For the sake of this introductory book, we will review the usual ways advisors earn compensation: in the form of mutual fund loads and commissions on stock trades. A discount broker may charge you $8 per stock trade, whereas a financial advisor can determine how much they charge you and this can be in the hundreds of dollars per trade. When a financial advisor recommends mutual funds to you, they will usually recommend loaded mutual funds that will generate a commission to the advisor. These commissions on mutual fund trades can be as high as 8.5%. For example, if you invest $100,000 into a loaded fund, the financial advisor may receive up to $8,500 in commission. This may seem like a lot of money, but remember that the financial advisor should be providing you a wealth of services that should ultimately benefit you.

Equally important, full-service brokerage firms often have hefty minimum balance requirements. In order to obtain the full benefits from the numerous services provided by a financial advisor, you will usually need to have quite a lot of assets to invest. For example, from my experience, most full-service brokerage firms have a minimum balance of $250,000. That's not to say that a full-service brokerage firm won't accept you as a client if you have less than $250,000, but it is unlikely.

So, for those of you with a larger asset base, you may want to consider a full-service broker if you want a hands off approach to your investments and are willing to accept higher fees and commissions. For those of us who either have a smaller asset base or want to manage our own investments, a discount broker would be a good place to start even if you have very little or no investment experience. As stated earlier, discount brokerages often provide very timely, accurate, and educational material that, if you take the time to review, could help you to become a better investor.

Summary

Understanding investments is one thing, but understanding how to participate in those investments is another. In order to participate in investing, you will generally work with two types of companies: *banks* and *brokerage firms*.

For the most part, banks are relatively easy to understand since most of us have experience working with banks. Typically, banks are in the business of lending money (e.g., housing and auto loans) and other non-investment related services, such as safety deposit boxes and cashier check issuance. The types of investments are usually exclusively within the cash asset class. Thus, with a bank, you will usually be able to participate in checking accounts, savings accounts, and certificates of deposit. If you want to participate in the other two asset classes (i.e., bonds and stocks), you will need to open an account with a brokerage firm.

Unlike banks, brokerage firms are not in the business of lending money. Instead, they are in the business of facilitating the trading of investments, including all three major asset classes. Essentially, there are the markets (e.g., the stock market) and the investor (you). How do you obtain access to these markets to buy stock or to purchase bonds? You use a brokerage firm, which acts as the middleman. There are two main types of brokerage firms: *discount* and *full-service.*

Discount brokerage firms are for the do-it-yourself investor who wants a hands on approach to investing. These investors typically know what they want to do and simply want the avenue to do it. With a discount brokerage firm, they get this avenue. Discount brokerage firms are usually online-based companies. You will open your account online, fund your account online, and place your own investment trades online. These types of firms may have a few physical branch locations, but for the most part, everything is done online.

It is because of this cost efficiency that these types of firms are able to offer you very affordable costs associated with investing. For example, we discussed commissions. Typically, when you buy and sell stocks, you will pay a commission. With discount brokerage firms, these commissions can be as low as a few dollars per trade. Also, there are often no fees associated with having an open account with a discount brokerage firm. However, they often will ask you to maintain a modest account balance (e.g., a few hundred dollars) but, in some instances, will have no balance requirement. This means you can have a trading account opened and simply transfer in funds when you want to start to invest.

Although discount brokerage firms are tailored to the do-it-yourself investor, they are great companies for novice investors as well. You will be able to open a cost-effective account, and even if you are new to investing, most of these discount brokerage firms have round-the-clock customer service staffed by licensed brokers. They may not be able to provide you with advice on what to buy or sell, but they can certainly guide you as to how to actually place trades through their online system. Also, these firms will usually devote considerable resources to providing you with educational material.

Full-service brokerage firms are for the investor who wants a hands off approach to investing. Typically, investors suitable for full-service brokerage companies want to hand their money off to a professional, usually a financial advisor, who will manage their investments for them. This includes initial asset allocation as well as on-going asset allocation. It is often expected that these financial advisors are up-to-date on the financial markets and will make necessary investment adjustments at their discretion. In addition to asset allocation, financial advisors will often provide a slew of other services, such as working with an investor's accountant during tax time and creating legacy planning (e.g., estate planning). It is because of these services that a full-service brokerage firm charges substantially higher fees than a do-it-yourself discount brokerage firm. Given the fee structure, as well as the number of services provided, it would not make much sense for an investor with a "small" asset base to open an account at a full-service brokerage firm. In fact, most full-service brokerage firms have minimum asset amounts required to open an account with them, and from my experience, that amount is usually around $250,000.

The investing world contains banks in which you can purchase cash-related investments and brokerage firms for all the asset classes. If you do not have the assets available for a full-service brokerage firm, or if you want to do it yourself, discount brokerage firms are a great option. In fact, I would urge you to open an account with a discount brokerage firm not only just to garner experience with how investment accounts work, but more importantly, to garner real-world investing experience. As you close this book and venture into the investing world to put into practice what we have been discussing, remember you can always come back here for reference!

Final Chapter
Closing Thoughts

We have spent the last few chapters of this book digesting quite a bit of information related to investing. We discussed the three main asset classes, retirement planning, investment taxation, and a host of other topics. For many of you, this may have been your first real introduction to investing. I want to sincerely thank you for having trusted me with your financial education.

At the beginning of this book, I shared with you my personal struggles, in my late teens, when learning the basics of investing. Unfortunately, my repeated attempts to learn the basics were discouraging at best. Real-world "financial professionals" mocked me. The beginner investing books I read were anything but beginner. Understanding even just the basics seemed out of my reach.

Over time, through determination, education, and real-world experience, I obtained knowledge of and skills with investments. I firmly believe the basics of investing aren't difficult if presented in understandable terms. Thus, my goal was to provide you with the absolute fundamentals of investing. It is my hope that you now have some inclination as to what investing entails, and you can branch off and start to delve deeper into specific areas that interest you. For example, we discussed how stocks are classified as either growth or value. Perhaps you will want to read up on that specific concept of stock investing. We also discussed asset allocation. Maybe you have a 401(k) and now want to make sure your asset allocation is appropriate, in which case you can start to review asset allocation strategies. I will be writing more books that cover each of these topics, but until then, it is my sincere hope that you now have an understanding of the basics and can start to engage in your own research on specific investing topics.

Before we part ways, I would like to reiterate some of the most important concepts you should take away from this book.

For the most part, when we invest, we are looking to grow our money—to earn a return. However, in order to grow our money, we need to be willing to assume some amount of risk and that risk usually revolves around the potential for us to lose some of our money. On one end, there are investments that will pose great amounts of risk, but also the potential for substantial return. On the other end, there are investments with minimal amounts of risk, yet very minimal potential of return. The age-old adage should be no surprise to us: *"The greater the risk, the greater the potential reward."*

As you venture out into the investing world, you will probably feel inundated with information. In particular, you may hear radio and television commercials, as well as friends and family members, discuss "investments" we have not covered in this book. I call these "outlier" investments and include things like real estate and precious metals (e.g., gold). Please, for the time being and until you garner more investment knowledge yourself, tread lightly with these discussions, and focus on the basics. Whatever you hear, I want you to remember that we classify investments into one of three asset classes: cash, bonds, or stocks. Yes, it really is this simple! Remember our buckets!

These buckets are a great way to remember this important aspect of investing. From this basic knowledge, you are now able to explain a few key characteristics of the asset classes. For example, we now know that cash is the most conservative asset class and stocks are the most aggressive (with bonds somewhere in the middle).

This basic understanding of the three asset classes will go a long way in solidifying and improving your knowledge of investing. However, recalling the buckets is not enough. You will need to be able to, and can now start to, explain what investments are contained within each asset class, as well as their corresponding risks and potential rewards, as presented in the following illustration:

The above concept (i.e., three buckets), along with the most common investments within each bucket, is the main idea I would like you to take away from this book. If you can recall the three asset classes and start to list the various investments within each asset class, my job is complete.

We learned that the main purpose of cash investments is to preserve your assets with the least amount of risk possible. Since cash investments do not pose much risk, the return (i.e., interest) on cash investments is usually quite small. Nevertheless, you can have confidence that the money you invest in a cash investment will be there when you need it.

What about bonds? One of the main goals of bond investments is to produce a substantially higher interest payment, or what is often referred to as *income*. Bonds introduce new and considerable risk when compared to cash investments. That is, the value of your bond investment can fluctuate up and down depending upon overall interest rate movements. Remember the teeter-totter illustration (page 46)? As interest rates increase, the value of a bond decreases (and vice versa). However, if you hold your bond until maturity, then you should expect to receive your initial investment back, regardless of interest rate movements.

The main goal of stock investing is growth of your principal amount invested. Unlike cash and bond investments, which aim to produce interest (i.e., income), stock investments are intended to produce capital gains. However, in pursuit of this growth, you might also experience losses, which is one of the main risks associated with stock investing. The potential to lose money in stocks is substantially higher than the other asset classes. Nonetheless, we learned that even within stocks, there are some that are more conservative than others. Remember our toilet paper versus electronics illustration (i.e., value and growth)?

Although we now have this new knowledge of the basics surrounding the three main asset classes, for many of us, actually choosing our own investments still seems quite daunting. For those, mutual funds and ETFs could be viable investment options. After all, with both mutual funds and ETFs, there is a management team who will invest our money on our behalf. Furthermore, this management team will continually monitor the investments and make changes as they deem necessary. You just sit back and hope the management team makes the right decisions for you.

No investment discussion would be complete without mentioning taxation. Tax laws are always changing, so it's imperative we consult competent tax advisors prior to making any investment decision, but we are now familiar with some of the basic concepts. These include capital gains and capital losses, as well as unrealized capital gains and unrealized capital losses. Just because you have an investment that, on paper, has decreased in value does not mean you have actually lost money. You need to sell your investment to *realize* a loss, or to realize a gain. You might be able to claim investment losses of up to $3,000 per year during tax filing, which could benefit you. On the other hand, if you make investment gains, you can expect to pay investment taxes. If you sell an investment within one year of purchase and make a gain, that gain will be treated as a *short-term capital gain* and subject to a higher capital gains tax rate. On the other hand, if you were to sell an investment after one year from purchase, then that gain will be treated as a *long-term capital gain* and subject to a lower capital gains tax rate.

There are accounts whose primary purpose is to shelter your investments from such taxation (e.g., capital gains, interest, and dividends). Two of the most widely known accounts are 401(k)s and Individual Retirement Accounts (IRAs). In addition to eliminating capital gains taxation (and in some instances deferred income taxation), these two accounts are crucial aspects of American retirement savings. Most of us will at some point have one or both of these accounts, so it's imperative we start to learn about them.

Simply, both IRAs and 401(k)s are nothing more than shelters in which you deposit your money. Once you deposit your money, you will then need to go inside those accounts and choose how to allocate your assets. Will you invest some of your money in cash, some in bonds, all of it in stocks, or some other combination?

On this note, another very important concept is *asset allocation*. It's one thing to know about the three asset classes, but it's another to decide how much of your money to invest in each. This is what the topic of asset allocation attempts to address. Although there are no perfect answers, there are certainly some rather useful rules of thumb. I would strongly encourage you to utilize the free online asset allocation tools I referenced in Chapter 7. At a minimum, "playing" around with these tools will provide you with further knowledge as to how you might decide to allocate your assets.

Finally, it is my sincere desire that you not only learned about the basics of investing, but that you will now venture out and attempt to actually engage in investing. In order to do this, you will most likely need to open an account either at a bank (for cash investments) or at a brokerage firm (for all three asset classes). Banks, for the most part, are straightforward. First, I imagine most of you already have bank accounts and so opening a new one with your bank should be rather easy. Otherwise, you can simply walk into a bank and ask to open an account; some banks even allow you to open accounts online. Brokerage accounts, on the other hand, can be a bit trickier.

First, there are two types of brokerage accounts: discount brokerage firms and full-service brokerage firms. Simply, if you have "a lot" of money to invest and want someone else to do the investing for you, then a full-service brokerage firm will probably be what you want to consider. At full-service brokerage firms, you will work with a financial intermediary, usually called a financial advisor, who works on your behalf. This financial intermediary will generally provide you with an array of services starting with the essentials of asset allocation (i.e., actually investing your money), as well as other services, such as tax planning and estate planning. It is because of this "royal treatment" that you will most likely pay more in fees and commissions as well as be required to have higher initial investment amounts.

For those of us with lower asset levels and/or for those of us who want to do things ourselves, discount brokerage firms are probably the way to go. Almost every aspect of a discount brokerage account is completed online: opening and funding accounts, transferring assets into and out of your account, placing investment trades, retrieving documents, etc.

This may sound like a lot since the responsibility to make these decisions and keep track of everything rests with you and not some financial intermediary. However, rest assured, most of these online discount brokerage firms make it as easy as possible to accomplish these tasks. In fact, most discount brokerage firms will have round-the-clock customer service that you can call whether you need help placing a trade or locating account statements. Additionally, many of these customer service centers will be able to spend great amounts of time with you, educating you on various financial topics.

However, since you have a discount brokerage account, most of these firms will not provide you with outright financial advice. In other words, you should not expect them to provide you with advice on asset allocation. Instead, most of these firms will have a wealth of online resources that, if you take advantage of them, will most assuredly help you further your investment knowledge. These resources can range from free asset allocation calculators to videos on the basics of stock investing and everything in between.

Additionally, many discount brokerage firms make it very affordable for you to open an account with them. Some may require only a few hundred dollars to open an account, and some may have no initial amount required. My suggestion is to give it a shot and open an account today. Start putting these investing principals into practice!

Once again, I want to sincerely thank you for trusting me with your financial education. I hope this book has allowed you to garner a new understanding of the basics of investing and opened your eyes to new and exciting investment possibilities. Please feel free to reference this book from time to time to help keep the fundamentals of investing fresh in your mind.

Keep an eye out for the companion series to this book that will introduce more advanced investing principals. These principals are all based on the foundations we have discussed and will include topics such as *short-selling* and *margin trading*, as well as more in-depth discussions on retirement planning (e.g., making your money work for you).

Also, feel free to reach out to me with any questions you might have, and I will respond to you as quickly as I can. I can be reached at info@ifreye.com.

Good luck with your future endeavors in investing!

Glossary

12(b)-1 – annual marketing or distribution fee on a mutual fund

401(k) – a retirement account to which employee and employer contribute, on which taxes are deferred until withdrawal, and for which the employee usually selects the types of investments

Aggressive – an investor willing to accept high levels of risk to maximize returns

Asset Allocation – the degree to which money is dispersed amongst the three asset classes based on an investors goals, risk tolerance, and time horizon

Back-End Load – a type of commission or fee an investor might pay when selling shares of a mutual fund

Bond Discount – a bond trades at a discount when it offers a coupon rate lower than prevailing interest rates

Bond – form of debt issued by corporations and government entities

Bond Premium – a bond trades at a premium when it offers a coupon rate higher than prevailing interest rates

Broker – an individual who usually receives commission for executing securities transactions on behalf of a customer

Brokerage Firm – a firm that conducts securities transactions on behalf of a client

Capital Gain – the positive difference between what a security was purchased for and subsequently sold for

Commission – the fee paid to a broker to execute a trade

Conservative – an investment strategy that seeks to preserve an investment's value by assuming low risk securities

Consumer Discretionary – goods and services considered non-essential by consumers, but desirable if income is sufficient to afford them

Consumer Staples – goods and services consumers are unwilling to cut out of their budget and are considered essential for day-to-day living such as medicine, food, and household items

Coupon Rate – yield paid by a fixed-income security and is synonymous with interest rate

Default Risk – the chance that companies or individuals will be unable to make the required payments on their debt obligations

Diversification – dividing invested money amongst different securities to minimize risk

Dividend – a payment made by a corporation to stock holders

Dow Jones Industrial Average® – a stock market index that tracks 30 actively traded, large cap stocks and is often times referred to as "*The Dow*" or "*The Dow Jones*"

Economic Contraction – a general slowdown in overall economic activity usually coupled with a decrease in employment, GDP, business profits, and household income

Economic Expansion – a period of economic growth as measured by a rise in real GDP as well as an increase in the level of economic activity

Equity – ownership interest in a company (i.e., stock)

ERISA – Legislation passed in 1974 that established a number of regulations to ensure that employers and other parties do not misuse retirement account funds

ETF – Exchange-traded fund

Expense Ratio – the proportion of assets required to pay annual operating expenses and management fees of a mutual fund

Federal Reserve Board – often times referred to as "The Fed" and is the main governing body of The Federal Reserve System

FICA – a tax on employees and employers that is used to fund the Social Security system

First-in, First-out (FIFO) – a method of reporting cost basis on a securities transaction that pairs the first shares purchased to the shares being sold

Financial Advisor – a professional, usually requiring licensing, offering financial advice to clients for a fee and/or commission

Front-End Load – a type of commission or fee an investor might pay when purchasing shares of a mutual fund

Gain – a profit realized when a security is sold for more than the security was purchased

Goals – an investor's financial objective

Index – measurement of the value of a section of a particular market (e.g., stock or bond market)

Inflation – the rate at which the general level of prices for goods and services is rising

Interest Rate Risk – the risk that an investment's value (e.g., bonds) will change due to a change in the absolute level of interest rates

Interest – the income derived from purchasing interest-paying investments

IRA – (Individual Retirement Account) a tax-deferred retirement plan

Last-in, First-out (LIFO) – a method of reporting cost basis on a securities transaction that pairs the last shares purchased to the shares being sold

Liquidity – how easily assets can be converted into cash

Load – the sales fee (i.e., commission) charged to an investor when purchasing or selling certain investments (e.g., mutual funds and annuities)

Long-term Capital Gain – the profit realized by selling an investment that has been held for longer than one year, usually subjected to lower taxation

Loss – receiving less money then what was initially invested

Maturity – the time when the issuer of a bond must repay the principal to an investor or when a borrower must repay a loan in full

NASDAQ® – (National Association of Securities Dealers Automated Quotation System) the largest electronic exchange in the world and a popular exchange for technology companies

No-Load – a mutual fund in which shares are bought and sold without a commission or fee being charged to the investor

NYSE – New York Stock Exchange; considered to be the largest equities-based exchange in the world located in New York City

Opportunity Risk – the loss arising when resources are committed for one opportunity and a better opportunity arises

PBGC – (Pension Benefit Guaranty Corporation) An independent agency of the United States government

Pension – sum of money paid regularly as a retirement benefit

Realized Gain – selling an investment for more than what the investment was purchased for

Realized Loss – selling an investment for less than what the investment was purchased for

Return – profit or loss on an investment, usually expressed as a percentage

Risk Level – the degree of volatility in investment returns that an investor is willing to tolerate

Risk – the uncertainty associated with an investment

S&P 500® – a stock market index tracking 500 of the largest companies within the United States (typically value-oriented companies)

SEP IRA – A retirement plan for a small business that does not maintain any other retirement plan for its employees

Share Specific Identification – a method of reporting cost basis on a securities transaction that allows the investor to report specific shares purchased to the actual shares being sold

Short-term Capital Gain – the profit on a sale of an investment that has been held for one year or less, usually results in higher taxation

SIMPLE IRA – A retirement plan for a small business with 100 or fewer employees

Speculation – a strategy of taking on significant risk of loss with the chance of a huge gain

Stock – ownership of a company indicated by shares, which represent a portion of the company's assets and earnings

Ticker – letter designation assigned to securities such as stocks and mutual funds

Unrealized Gain – the increased market value of an asset that is still being held, often times referred to as a *Paper Gain*

Unrealized Loss – the decreased value of an investment that is still being held, often times referred to as a *Paper Loss*

Volatility – the amount of uncertainty or risk regarding the changes in value of a particular investment

Yield – the percentage return paid in the form of a dividend for a stock investment or the rate of interest paid on a bond

Made in the USA
Columbia, SC
24 December 2017